Are You Love Smart or Love Stupid?

DEBUNKING THE MYTHS THAT STOP YOU FROM FINDING AND KEEPING LOVE

Are You Love Smart or Love Stupid?

DEBUNKING THE MYTHS THAT STOP YOU FROM FINDING AND KEEPING LOVE

DR. RACHEL SIMS

Library of Congress Cataloging-in-Publication Data has been applied for

ISBN: 979-8-9852834-0-2

Cover and layout design by Pfeifer Design

Creative License Publishing, LLC.
https://www.creativelicensepublishing.com

TABLE OF CONTENTS

INTRODUCTION

One day, I ran to my favorite coffee shop to grab an afternoon cup. Three more patients and a night full of dissertation work required a certain amount of caffeine. With my iced drink nestled in its holder, I pulled my car out of its parking space and up to the stoplight, just as the deep voice of a local talk show host welcomed his new caller. I turned up the volume.

"Hey man, give me your name and tell us your relationship issue."

"Hi, my name is Todd, and I don't have a problem. I just wanted to offer your last caller some advice my uncle gave me."

I rolled my eyes and grabbed my cup out of the cupholder.

"For those of you just tuning in, our last caller wanted to know how to get a guy at work to notice her. Ok Todd, what's your advice?"

"Dating is like a fart. If you try to force it, all you get is shit. If you just let it happen, then it all comes out fine."

I spat my coffee all over my lap and grabbed for the napkin on my passenger seat.

"Wow, never heard it put that way," the host said, laughing, "I can only imagine what your uncle's take on marriage is."

"He says to date the Ferrari, marry the Volvo."

'What!" I screamed out loud to myself.

"How so, Todd?"

Oh, this host needs to cut him off, not encourage him! I thought.

"He says the Ferrari may be sexy, but they're high maintenance and temperamental. The Volvo's are reliable and safe. That's why I'm focusing on dating 10's right now. Eventually, I will look for that mediocre girl with a good personality to marry."

The host and I simultaneously asked, "How old are you?"

"18."

I threw my car in park outside my office, shut off the radio, and said, "Get this kid a therapist; he's going to need it!"

Understand, I am not bashing this kid or his uncle. I believe the uncle's intentions were good, just like anyone's friend or family member who freely gives their opinions. People in our life want for us what we want for ourselves, love and happiness. However, sometimes the advice, although well-intentioned, can be misguided.

How do I know? Well, I'm both a therapist and the recipient of advice I wished I'd never listened to. If I could go back in time and tell my younger self what to do and what not to do, I would go in a heartbeat. But, since I haven't yet figured out time travel, I want to give others the wisdom I've learned through study and experience in my professional life and my own search for love.

Throughout this book, I will share situations that have happened to my patients and others I've met. The names and many of the details of the stories have been altered to protect all those involved. Sharing real-life examples will help me explain today's environment and how you can *uncomplicate* your search for lasting love.

Clearly, since you've picked up this book, you've admitted your need for help in finding or keeping love. Please, continue reading and get ready to learn about the origins of love, how technology isn't always our friend, and which dating myths, advice, or rules to keep, and which to throw in the trash. Then, I will simplify the process of discovering and maintaining a healthy and happy relationship.

Chapter 1 –
All About Love

The irony that I began writing the first chapter of this book on Valentine's Day was not lost on me. A holiday marketed as a day devoted to romance has little to do with real love. Love isn't buying someone a box of chocolates once a year. But just like Forest Gump compared a box of chocolates to life, you can say the same for love; "…you never know what you're gonna get." Love isn't a dozen roses, although, like a rose, love has its prickly parts. And love isn't a card written by Hallmark, but it is about expressing how you feel. Above all else, love shouldn't be celebrated once a year; it should be a daily event.

But the truth is, many people struggle with love on a day-to-day basis. Whether someone is looking for a date or trying to hold onto a marriage that has spanned decades, there are often more questions than answers. This ongoing search for help has led to many books on the subject.

One of the most notable books on love and romance came out in the early 1990s. John Gray published a book called *Men are From Mars, Women are From Venus*, which went on to be a national bestseller. The entire premise of the book is about how men and women are emotionally different. And, according to Gray, understanding each other's differences will improve our communication and relationships.

There are some truths there: Like when you are angry with your boyfriend, he doesn't notice. Or when you just want to be held, but your lover thinks you want sex. Partners don't always talk the same language. However, I disagree with the theory that gender explains every difference or communication breakdown in a relationship. Who you are as a person and lover also impacts how people interact with one another. And those characteristics are a combination of what you are born with, the environment you were raised in, the world today, and others' advice. Your differences aren't just related to your sex.

"Love is a lot like a toothache, it doesn't show up
on x-rays, but you know it's there."
– George Burns

Where We Learn About Love: Nature and Nurture

Each child is born with specific characteristics, nature. And each child is raised in an environment that is distinct to their family and surroundings, nurture. You take nature and mix it with nurture, and it produces a unique human being. Like snowflakes, no two people are exactly alike—no matter your gender or sexual orientation.

And from birth onward, you are in a constant state of learning, including developing your ideas about love. Most don't stop to think about times when their parents held hands in front of them, hugged them, or read them a book as being lessons on love. But it is the sum of those million little moments, some good and some perhaps not, that make up one's love education.

By the time we hit adulthood and seek a romantic partner, the process can be pretty revealing. This time can illuminate who we are as lovers, our ability to love ourselves, what we've learned about love in general, and how we both give and receive love. But it's not just nature and nurture that make us the lovers we are. Changes in society and our adult experiences also alter our perceptions and expectations.

"If we meet offline, and you look nothing like your pics,
you're buying me drinks until you do."
– Unknown

Love in Modern Day – Dating Apps/Social Media

Recently, I had two patients, Joe and Kristin, a divorced couple working on their relationship as co-parents. These two continue to live together for the sake of their kids. Yet, Joe and Kristin actively seek dates on a well-known dating app and, oddly enough, confide in each other about their experiences. Each night, after they put the kids to bed, they swap stories about who each is talking to and any potential dates they have coming up.

"Hey, I just got a message from this girl," Joe said, sitting on the couch next to Kristin.

"Let me hear it."

Joe reads, "Hi, I'm Janice. I don't mean to disrespect you, but I'm looking for an honest and trustworthy boy. I'm ready to spoil you with an allowance. I can afford to start with $400 weekly, so if you're interested, please call me."

"$400 bucks?" Kristin asked, laughing hysterically.

I listened to them retell this story in one of our sessions. Despite being impressed by how these two learned to co-parent peacefully, I shook my head in disbelief. It never fails to amaze me how people connect with someone romantically and how wrong they can be. And I wonder: Is it all just a combination of who they are and what they've learned growing up? Or have their views changed along with the advancements in technology? I believe it is a combination of past and present. But here's a critical point: You can't change your history, but you can change how you deal with your current situation.

The world today pushes ideas of immediacy and perfectionism. If we need something, we order it online, and it can be in our hands in less than 24 hours. If we want to know something, we just Google it, and the answers are in front of us. And thanks to social media, television, and movies, we are led to believe we can obtain perfection in every aspect of our lives. The idea that we can have it *all*, and we can have it *now*, has been infused into our brains like tea in hot water. These are both false and dangerous assumptions when applied to one's quest for love.

Using dating apps is a lot like selling a home. Before you place that "For-Sale" sign on your front lawn, your house needs to look like something Chip and Joanna whipped up on HGTV. The same is true for dating profiles. No one posts pictures of themselves with food in their teeth or their hair uncombed. Nor will a bio state someone is jobless and living with Grandma and her four cats. Like you stage a home for sale, the information and pictures on dating apps are doctored or tweaked to sell the dream. Buyer beware. Make the connection, but don't assume he or she is as perfect as they seem.

Think of the posts you "like" on social media sites: A friend posts pictures of her and her boyfriend in sexy swimwear, tan, and smiling, with the crystal blue waters of the Caribbean in the background. Your cousin, her husband, and their three cherubs on the beach at sunset, all dressed alike and posing as if they're in a Gap ad. And the words below each picture include the eye-roll-inducing "#Blessed." Do you think these images and words can change how you look at yourself and your relationship? Yes, they can, and they do, even if you don't realize it.

With all the media and social media's attention on perfectionism, people today are harder on themselves than ever. It needs to stop. More than anything else in my practice, I've noticed that individuals must learn to love themselves before seeking a romantic partner. I'm not talking about arrogance. I'm talking about loving who you are inside and out. If you can't appreciate all your qualities, then how can you expect someone else to? The journey to self-love is different for everyone. It all starts with changing your expectations and dispensing with the idea of perfection as the goal.

If this is a struggle for you, seek help, preferably from a professional who can give you personalized assistance. Remember, you attract what you project. Work on what you are putting out to the world first, and your romantic pursuits will fall in line with your goals.

Maggie hopped in the car after yet another engagement party. She scanned Instagram and thought about how the mother of the bride-to-be had assured her, "You're next, Maggie!" But she started to feel her boyfriend of three years, Steve, may never commit to anything but his lifted F-150 or the four-wheeler he's done nothing but talk about for weeks.

The envy ate away at her as Steve asked, "What was all that random crap of fruit and cheese? I'm starving!"

"It was a charcuterie table!" Maggie snipped as she scrolled through her friend's endless posts with her sparkling diamond, strategically positioned in each photo.

An hour later, Steve was raiding the fridge and making a sandwich, while Maggie's emotions churned, "Want one, he asks?"

"A ring? A commitment?"

Steve laughed, "No, a sandwich. Aren't you hungry?"

Maggie, fighting a combination of tears and rage, put down her phone, walked over to the bread, held up the end piece of a long loaf of Wonder, "You know what I am? I'm this end piece, the piece that no one wants unless they're completely out of options and they're starving!"

"What are you talking about?" Steve asked, stacking his snack a mile high.

"I'm talking about being the last one picked in dodgeball growing up, the last one to get boobs, and now I'll be the last one to get engaged! "You just don't get it! Just leave!"

Steve grabbed his giant sandwich and calmly walked to the front door and then turned to Maggie, "When you get back to being you, call me."

Maggie slammed the front door shut and burst into tears.

This is just one of the millions of scenarios where one's expectations about love come from the barrage of messages passed through media, social media, advice, or small comments from others. And as I've said, that information can frequently be false or misinterpreted. Yet, it's that tainted knowledge that spurs emotions and causes one to make rash decisions, not unlike Maggie's choice to throw Steve out of her house.

"Take my advice, I don't use it anyway." - Anonymous

Love Advice – Deciphering Good from Bad

No man or woman is perfect, and neither is any relationship. So, I have some suggestions to save your sanity for the non-committed adults who receive an abundance of advice from friends and family. First, take a step back and learn to consciously filter what you see and hear. You do this by reminding yourself that what we see and hear is not always 100% reality. To determine facts from fiction, you must focus on the advice givers' motivation. To understand what I mean by motivation, let's revisit the previous scenario of Maggie and Steve from the point after Steve walked out.

Maggie sat curled up on her couch, downing a bag of Cheetos when she received a phone call. Although she wanted to answer and yell out how annoyed, hurt, and angry she was with Steve, she first looked at the caller ID. It was her friend Janet. Gorgeous, successful, and eternally-single Janet never understood why Maggie would want a steady boyfriend. Maggie's finger hovered over the green button for a second, and then she sent the call to voicemail.

The phone rang again fifteen minutes later. This time it was Julie. Julie's most significant achievement in life was how long she managed to stay single with no prospects in sight. Despite paying for multiple dating apps, perpetually lonely Julie hasn't had a successful date yet. Julie personified misery loves company, and she would only rant about how wrong Steve was and that he didn't deserve her friend. Maggie muted the ringer.

Maggie got off the couch and grabbed a carton of Ben and Jerry's and a spoon. But before she made it back to the dent in her crumb-covered sofa, her phone vibrated against the glass coffee table. It was Angela. Angela was the habitual dater and always trying to get Maggie to play the field, saying, "You don't know what you're missing out on!" Again, Maggie ignored the call.

The fourth and final time her phone rang, Maggie answered. It was her friend from work, Casey.

"Hey, what's up?"

Maggie sniffled out, "Not much."

"You're lying. I can tell you've been crying. Which probably means your stuffing your face and watching *Bridget Jones' Diary* again."

"Yep."

"I knew today's engagement party would be tough. Did you and Steve fight?"

"Kind of. Well, I yelled, and he looked at me like I was nuts."

"Get a grip. Pull yourself together and talk to him. You need to tell Steve how you feel, and I mean *really* feel. Stop the passive-aggressive crap and have a good heart to heart."

What made Maggie pick up the last call and avoid the others? What would you have done if you were Maggie? Although Maggie let her expectations about an engagement get the better of her, she thoughtfully contemplated each caller's potential motives. Ultimately, she chose Casey, who shared an unbiased and mature perspective.

Each of Maggie's initial three callers represent a type of friend you should avoid seeking advice from. First, there is Janet, the perpetually single, type-A friend. This type of friend is a walking billboard promoting their belief that being single is best. Next is Julie, the always single, type-B friend who wants everyone to be lonely and miserable like her. The third type is Angela, the over-achiever in dating. Her happy-go-lucky attitude and carefree outlook on relationships will try to convince you that there are more fish in the sea.

And if you think I would suggest going to the family for advice, you would be wrong. Your family loves you and wants the best for you, and that is precisely the problem. These desires diminish their ability to be objective, see the other side of the coin, and effectively guide you to the desired result. Lastly, never, under any circumstances, talk to the ex. I've had patients who have gone down that path only to convince themselves they still have feelings for these individuals. They forget all the reasons they broke it off with them previously. It's a slippery slope and one that almost always ends badly.

People, it's time to uncomplicate your love life. Expectations fueled by society's desire for perfectionism can be reframed. And when well-meaning friends and family impart their wisdom through myths and theories, you can filter out the good from the bad. This book will give you the much-needed tools to finding and keeping love in the modern day.

Chapter 2 –
Dating Myths

One night, while dining with some friends, I became distracted by three women sitting at an adjacent table. They were in their mid to late 20's, not much younger than us. Still, something about this different group and their interaction piqued my interest. I will confess that I did eavesdrop, but in my defense, they weren't talking in hushed tones.

"Can you believe that?" a woman, clearly the youngest of the group, who resembled a grown-up version of Cindy Lou Who, from *The Grinch Who Stole Christmas*, asked. She then took a long, delicate sip from her glass of rosé. I will refer to her from this point on as Cindy.

"I told you, I didn't think he would be right for you. You need to be more discerning." The seemingly picky, dark-haired woman retorted before grabbing for the breadbasket. I suspected she substituted emotional connection with carbs, but it did nothing to enhance her disposition. She seemed to dawn a permanent scowl in direct contrast to Cindy Lou's big blue eyes and painted-on smile. I will refer to her as friend number two.

Friend number three bore a striking resemblance to a wind-blown version of Lady Gaga. She pointed at Cindy and said in her deep, scratchy voice, attempting to understand the conversation, "You dated Porsche-guy last night? Guys with fancy cars are notoriously cheap. I told you, never date a guy with a nice car."

"He took her to Sheetz for a steak sandwich!" Picky friend number two interjected.

"The steak was good, but then he let me pay for both of us!" Cindy exclaimed before taking another long sip of wine, which she proceeded to spill on her Lily Pulitzer sundress.

"Well, chalk him up to gone and move on!" Lady Gaga said, grabbing her drink and signaling the waiter for another.

"Earth to Rachel," my group said in unison as I looked up to see the waiter standing over me, pad in hand and slightly annoyed.

"Oh, sorry, I'll have the chicken," I answered.

Two seconds after handing the waiter my menu, I heard, "You had sex with him?" Lady Gaga shouted for the entire restaurant to hear.

Cindy turned beet red as friend number two offered her opinion wielding a half-eaten roll in her hand, "You should never have sex with a guy on the third date. You have to wait three months before you give it up."

"Maybe you should give it up a little more," Lady Gaga said, looking at friend number two and grabbing her drink from the waiter.

I resisted the temptation to leave my card on their table as we left the restaurant. I've heard it all as a marriage and relationship therapist. My sessions are riddled with statements like: "My mother says that I'll never find Mr. Right if I wear blue eye-shadow." "My sister says to bring a list of questions on any first date. If the guy doesn't give me the answers I want, I move on before dessert is served." "The guy I work out with every other Saturday swears to get a girl, you need to be a jerk."

And then I have those patients that make up their own "no-fail" rules like: "I never date a woman who can't be dropped off on the side of the road and get herself home. She needs to be a cross between Bear Grylls and Jennifer Aniston." "I will only go on a second date if the guy is ready to commit." "If a woman wants me to treat her as an equal, she better pay half for dinner!" And I can't help but wonder why we make finding and keeping love more complicated than it needs to be.

Time to debunk the advice and myths floating around! Time to uncomplicate love!

"Love is like taking a walk in the park. Jurassic Park."
– Anonymous

Dating Myths

Myth #1: Your perfect match is out there

You're at another dreaded family dinner party where everyone is married or is about to be, and you're search for Mr. Right is as dry as the Mojave Desert. You slink over to the appetizer table, dodging your Aunt Kathy, and balance your drink in one hand while grabbing for the salami and cream cheese rolls.

"Ah, once pass the lips, forever on the hips!" Aunt Kathy sings, as she sneaks up on your left side. You go to move down, but your older, married sister shows up on your right side. "So, are you dating anyone?"

Your sister chimes in, "Nope, she's still single."

Aunt Kathy puts you in a big hug, "Oh darling, Mr. Right is out there for you. Don't give up hope. It's not like you're thirty yet."

Your sister bursts out laughing and walks away. You smile at Aunt Kathy, thinking, *I turned thirty, three years ago.*

From the time you were little, you received the message, explicitly and implicitly, that there is one person out there who is meant just for you and perfect. Whether you heard it at home, at school, or saw it on almost every Disney film, this idea of the perfect mate was delivered to you with a big red bow. And at the risk of sounding blunt, I am here to tell you there is no such person as a perfect partner or match. Just as oil doesn't mix with water, perfection doesn't exist in reality.

As an individual, if you cannot separate what is pretend and unattainable from the truth, you create unreal expectations on both ends. This makes you look for perfection in another and yourself. Expecting that you or your life should look like a doctored Instagram post or a Hollywood creation is a lot of pressure to start your search for a potential mate. So, let's cut to the chase: you are not perfect, and neither is anyone else.

Once you dial down your expectations, you will open yourself up to the possibility of finding a suitable mate or partner in life. Maybe they won't look like Bradley Cooper, cook like Wolfgang Puck, earn more than Jeff Bezos, and have Matthew McConaughey's charm. Still, they may stimulate you emotionally, physically, and spiritually to enhance your life. And shouldn't that be the goal? Shouldn't a relationship make your life better, not fulfill some ideal you've created in your mind?

I am not pushing the concept of just accept anyone or settling. But I am saying the expectation of perfection isn't attainable. So, perhaps happiness lies somewhere in the middle.

Donald Winnicott, a pediatrician, developed the "good enough" theory concerning mothers and their children. This theory incorporated Freud's theory of introjection. Introjection is when we take on others' attitudes while suppressing our own as a means of survival. His concept centered around a mother's desire to be perfect as defined by society. Winnicott's theory states that being "good enough" is optimal, since perfection doesn't exist, and a mother's failures are beneficial to the child. And by fail, he means something the child can overcome (2009). For example, if the child wants a snack but the mother doesn't have one prepared, the child must wait or get the snack themself. The mother's imperfection is preparing the child for life.

So, can you apply the "good enough" theory to a partner? Yes, because we need to stop expecting perfection because, as I've said, it doesn't exist in any human. Also, the theory of "good enough" focuses on realistic expectations as being the apex.

What am I suggesting you do? First, write down all the characteristics you would want someone to possess, such as athletic, honest, compassionate, financially independent, and motivated. Review that list carefully and circle which attributes are most important to you. Then identify those qualities that you can overlook if they aren't there and put a line through them. Now you will have a list that addresses your needs.

Takeaway: Finding someone to date can be like buying your first new car on a budget. You want all the options, but you need to decide which ones are most important. You may say yes to air conditioning, no to lighted cupholders—yes to loyal, no to hair like Patrick Dempsey. Before you start your search for a mate, be genuine and honest with yourself. What are the things that matter and the things that don't? Move your expectations away from perfection towards something more realistic.

Myth #2: Love should be easy

You've been on three dates with someone new, and you are full of excitement. You wake up, and even your hairy, sweaty, drooling dog smells like rose petals. Your new person texts you before you get out from under the covers to let you know they are thinking about you. You smile, clutching the phone to your chest, and think *I've found my soulmate. This is how it's supposed to be!*

Wake up and smell the coffee! You are in the euphoric beginning stages of romance. It should be light and easy at this stage, but this will not represent your relationship in the long term. Famed psychotherapists and love researchers, John Gottman, Ph.D., and Julie Gottman, Ph.D., claim there are three stages of love. The three stages are the romantic stage (the easy stage), the individuation stage, and the mature love stage (Gottman, n.d.).

In the romantic love stage, the individuals are over-the-moon happy. Their bodies are flooded with hormones that make them practically addicted to each other. It's also the stage where fantasies and idealizations are applied, and they start envisioning the other person as "the one." This stage appears intoxicatingly easy and makes each person feel as if it will never end. Romantic love is what feel-good romance movies are about—you know, the ones that end with a passionate kiss and the assumption that the two will live happily ever after.

But that's not entirely true. That is not to say a person won't be happy after the romantic stage, just not to the same excitement level. And quite often, this is where the myth that love should be easy comes from. Shouldn't we feel this happy and excited all the time? Sure, but it's not reality, despite what Hollywood presents to us.

In the next stage, called the individuation stage, the concoction of hormones flooding in declines, and the other person's idealizations fade. Each partner gains a more realistic vision of the other. How he snorts in his sleep is no longer cute, the way she flosses her teeth suddenly grosses you out, or you both stop closing the bathroom door as you do your business, are examples of a couple moving into the next stage of love.

This individuation stage is where conflicts surface. When there are two individuals, conflict is bound to happen since no two people will agree on everything, no matter how compatible they are. This stage can last months, years, and even decades, depending on the lovers and the context of their relationship. It's also the time when there is a higher probability of the relationship ending.

If the couple weathers the individuation stage, they move on to the mature love stage. This time is when both people have primarily made space for one another. There is a higher existence of safety, connection, and acceptance. Conflict does not get eliminated at this point, nor does the couple revert to the ease of the romance stage. Work and conflict resolution are still necessary, but they are taken as a matter of course. Their trust in the relationship is much stronger.

Takeaway: Just as you don't buy a dog just to be your running partner, you don't start a committed relationship to have a date on Saturday nights. Love and commitment require attention. Don't go into any relationship thinking it's only suitable when it's easy—this is truly a myth. Anticipate the work and be prepared to give of yourself.

Connection and communication are two key components that every romantic partnership must have to be successful. Make time for one another to keep your connection alive. And communicate often and openly. Stop expecting your partner to telepathically interpret your feelings. Be genuine in expressing yourself, but respectful to your partner's words as well. Remember, everything is a two-way street.

We will discuss the importance of connecting and communicating with your partner further on in the book.

Myth #3: Always play hard to get

Sally and her friend Mark were walking down the street. A guy she had a massive crush on was headed straight for them. Mark elbowed her, "Twelve o'clock. Your obsession is headed for us."

"I know," she snapped under her breath as the hottie from three floors down got closer. Sally felt her face getting warmer. He's almost within feet of them when Sally said, "Hi, nice day out, right?"

Her neighbor stopped and nodded, trying to think of where he knew her from.

Sally realized this and stumbled over her own words, "Um, I'm Sally from 6. Um, 6C. You know, um, where you live. Not that I've been stalking you or anything, I—."

He cut her off, "Oh yeah. Hi." He looked at his watch, gave a wave, and kept going.

"Smooth," Mark commented, "You might try to play a little hard to get next time. Try and avoid the 'hey, I'm psycho neighbor' approach."

What would you have done if you were Sally? Was Mark right in his advice? What if I said Sally was on to something, but her execution failed? What if I told you, you should walk up to the person you're interested in and tell them how you feel, then ask if they'd like to go on a date?

I feel your eyes rolling as you read the previous question. And yes, I just asked you to do the unthinkable. Why? Because why not? Any of the other above options are just part of game playing. Think about it, if the other person responds to your game playing, doesn't that increase the likelihood they are a player? Yes, and is there a solid future with someone like that? Probably not.

I once went to see my therapist and told her about a guy I liked, but I didn't know if he shared my feelings. That's when she said, "Tell him how you feel."

Honestly, this advice caught me off guard too, and initially, I resisted it.

But, per usual, my therapist posed an interesting question, "What do you have to lose? If he's not interested, he walks away thinking you are an honest person; a person who says how she feels, and who goes after what she wants." It all made sense at that point. It didn't take away my fear of doing it and potentially being embarrassed by his rejection. It did, however, exemplify how ridiculous the process of waiting to see if he would show any interest in me genuinely was.

Many single individuals spend excessive time thinking about someone they would like to date, without ever thinking to approach the person to ask them out. I have patients and friends who all have wondered about and watched the object of their affections from afar. This process never got them anywhere.

Let's play the what-if game: What if you say, "Hi, my name is X. I see you walk by each day, and I was wondering if you would be interested in having a drink sometime?" They will have one of two primary responses: "Thank you, but I am not interested." Or "Thank you for asking. I'd love to go." If they don't take you up on it, at least you've answered your question and allowed yourself the opportunity to move on. If they say yes, then you have a date!

Now, reverse the positions, and instead of pursuing someone, someone is trying to get a date with you? How would you handle it? Still play hard to get?

Mary sat at a bar with her friends. A random guy came up to her, "You think I work for FedEx?"

Confused, Mary looked up, "No, why do you say that?"

"Because I've seen you checking out my package."

Mary gave a nervous laugh before coming back, "How old is that cheesy line?"

The guy smiled, and his face lit up, "Longer than you've been old enough to drink. My name is Jack." He laughed and held out his hand to shake. After sharing some laughs, Jack asked a non-committal Mary out several times. They eventually went their separate ways after exchanging numbers.

A few days later, Mary was out with her same group of friends, and Jack texted her to ask her out. Her friends simultaneously said, "Do not text him back for at least two days!"

When your friends tell you to play hard to get, do you? Well, that is entirely up to you as you may enjoy the cat and mouse game. After all, it can be fun and exciting to think someone is interested in you and that you hold the cards. Be warned, here are the possible resulting scenarios of the above example:

- If Mary takes too long, Jack will move on.
- If Mary plays the game but gives in too soon, they may have some brief fun until Jack gets bored. A man who likes the chase won't date for long. He's not long-term material.

Understand that players play for a reason. Although that reason depends on the player themselves, the inevitable outcome is the same—they aren't around for the long haul. I am not suggesting Mary never date this guy. I am merely saying if she likes him, to proceed with caution—knowledge is power.

There are other typical clichés associated with this playing hard-to-get myth:

- Putting the person down will get them interested.
- Make them jealous.
- Let them make the first move.

Any of these statements are also untrue. If you put someone down or try to make them jealous and they keep responding, you can assume the game is working for them—they are a player. Suppose you decide to wait for them to make the first move. In that case, you're back at the waiting and wondering game, and as I explained earlier, it's just a colossal waste of your time and energy. Games are for parties or family time. If you like someone, being upfront and confident is the best approach.

Takeaway: How many times after losing at a board game have you heard the winner declare, "Hate the game, not the player?" But in the game of love, you *will* hate "the player" in the end. If you want a mature, lasting relationship, be direct and love yourself enough not to waste your time being a player or being played.

Myth #4: Opposites attract or look for sameness

Cameron flopped on her couch and checked her phone. There is a message waiting for her on her dating app. She opened it:

"Do you hate men? Your haircut advertises that to us, just to let you know."

Cameron touched her short hair, laughed, and typed a response:

"If you got all that from my haircut, hate to see what you get out of actually meeting me?"

The guy responded immediately:

"LOL…I don't know. You're brave enough to respond, and life is a learning process. You're not my usual type, but hey, I like to be humbled when I'm wrong. Educate me? I am kinda sweet, and I'd love to cook you dinner and buy you flowers."

She shook her head and wondered: *Is this guy for real?* But she decided to type a response that would end this horrible conversation:

"I hate flowers, probably as much as I hate men."

The saying "opposites attract" is probably the most significant falsehood that drives almost every rom-com in the movie industry. It's a fact that positive and negative forces allow for electricity to flow. However, this scientific fact is not valid for human "electricity" or attraction. Does this make the advice that you should find a partner who is just like you correct? Not necessarily, but the later theory does hold some water.

One study revealed that 80% of us believe that opposites attract, thank you, Hollywood. However, more recent research disproves this theory by tracking the digital footprint of its participants. The study showed that people seeking love online chose, with greater frequency, individuals who shared similar interests and beliefs (Smith, 2017).

Psychologist Donn Byrne was one of the first psychologists or sociologists to study the impact of sameness in choosing a mate. Byrne created a method of testing known as the "Phantom Stranger Technique" (Swami, 2017). This process started by asking individuals enrolled in the study to complete a questionnaire. The survey assessed their attitudes on a wide range of topics impacting the world. Next, Byrne gave each participant, unbeknownst to them, a fictitious person's answers to the same survey they'd just taken and asked them to evaluate them. The results: individuals showed higher attraction levels for the "phantom strangers" who had similar views.

If psychologists, like Donn Byrne, are believed, we are more attracted to sameness than differences. Although, the myth that opposites attract makes for good storylines, in real life, that rarely happens.

On the contrary, I have met some individuals who claim the relationship works because they married someone unlike themselves. Do I think these individuals are lying? No, but I do believe the interpretation of "opposite" is incorrect. For example, say you hate sports, but your partner loves sports. Or you are messy, but your mate is a neat freak. These are examples of differences, but do they make you opposites? No. If your attitudes or beliefs that truly matter are the same, but the trivial or less important things are different, you're not opposites in a relationship.

To exemplify my hypothesis, let's take the movie that constantly plays on multiple cable channels, *Sweet Home Alabama*. In this movie, Reese Witherspoon and Josh Lucas were exes destined to be together, but their "differences" drove them apart. She wanted to leave small-town America for bigger and better. He wanted to stay in his hometown and live a quiet life. The movie would have you believe their opposite attraction is so intense they get back together. The truth is, it's the sameness or similar core values that drive Reece and Josh's characters back together. Their love of their past, hometown, family, and friends, pulls them back together. Their core similarities brought them together, not some negative-positive electrical pull.

Does the debunking of opposites attract give credence to the cliché that you should find someone just like you? No, not necessarily. Finding someone who has all the same likes and dislikes as you and agrees with you on literally everything may seem like a dream partner in life—in reality, not so much.

Lovers that appear to be the same in every way, outwardly and inward, may seem perfect for one another. Still, quite often, there is little physical or emotional attraction. Psychologist Arthur Aron claims that individuals who hold *too many* similarities between them can derail any romantic interest. Aron attributes this truth to the absence of a "growth factor."

That is to say, that when two people are exactly alike, they aren't likely to ever leave their comfort zones, and they lack the "growth factor." This situation often causes the relationship to stagnate—a too much of a good thing scenario. Now, individuals who appear different on the surface might be attracted to each other because they may be similar at the core, but their outward differences provide growth opportunities. I once heard about a couple, identical in their beliefs, but one loved skiing and the other golf. And after their first year together, both picked up a new hobby, which made their connection stronger—same but different, equals happiness.

Takeaway: Peanut butter and jelly or salt and pepper are perfect together. And despite their outward differences, they enhance each other. In humans, it's the same concept. We are not attracted to our mates because of differences. We are drawn together because of core similarities. However, it's our differences that make each of us better when we are together. Look for individuals who allow you to grow but, at the core, share your values.

Myth #5: Age isn't a factor

My patient, Mike, sat in his usual chair with his right leg nervously shaking while he fixed the collar on his plaid shirt, the same one my dad owned. Mike was 23.

"Mike, tell me about your new love."

His leg stopped shaking, and his eyes lit up, "It's awesome. She gets me. We're both foodies and love minigolf. She's the first woman I've dated."

"Well, you've dated other women. What about Carol or Margie?"

"They were girls. Allison is the first *woman* I've dated. But…"

I sat back, giving him time to process his thought. Mike was highly mature beyond his years, yet connecting with people his age presented a challenge—it's why he sought my help. Superior intelligence and an old soul worked against him despite his sweet, kind personality. "But?"

"Well, she's getting negative attitudes from her kids and her friends, and it's bothering her. I'm afraid she's going to call it quits."

"Ok." I gave him time to continue before I jumped in with more questions—active listening.

"I haven't said anything because I was afraid you wouldn't approve either. You know, given my issues with my mom." Mike tilted his head for emphasis, but after a long pause, he let it out, "Allison is 43."

Let's talk about May-December romances, like Mike and Allison's. Should you pursue a relationship with someone much older or younger than you? I don't subscribe to the theory that age should be a red flag. I eventually explained that to Mike too. When you find someone who meets all your essential criteria and you genuinely like being with them, be open to a relationship. Any age difference that may exists shouldn't present a roadblock.

Most issues with a May-December romance come from the people *outside* the relationship, projected onto the people *in* the relationship. Therefore, before you date someone with a sizeable age gap between you, the most important thing is to anticipate others' curiosity and opinions. Some of the topics that will arise are:

- Younger individuals are immature.
- Older individuals are creepy.
- You won't have anything in common.
- You won't get each other's references.
- You have mother or father issues. That's why you're together.
- You or they could be labeled "gold-digger."

Let's address each one of the above points with facts:

- Immaturity can occur when there is an age gap or not. Immaturity is dependent on the individual, not on their numeric age.

- On the flip side, the older partner is often assumed by others outside the relationship as creepy. Creepy, like maturity, doesn't hold a one-to-one correlation with age—it's all dependent upon the individual involved.
- If you can't understand the other's references from time to time, look them up. Educate yourself.
- When others judge your relationship by saying you have mommy or daddy issues for being with someone older, it's just their opinion.
- Just as the label of someone having mommy or daddy issues, the term 'gold-digger is sometimes imposed by others. Only you know the reasons you are in a relationship.

Takeaway: Road-ragers not-withstanding, if someone cuts you off on the free-way, you yell at them or blow your horn and move on. Why can't we do that when people question our relationships? If you and your partner are fulfilled in the relationship or you like someone with an age gap, age shouldn't be a deal-breaker because of what others will say. Assess the motives in others' comments and make the best decision for you and your partner.

Myth #6: Lower your expectations

The phrase "lower your expectations" equates to lowering the standards of what you think you deserve. Please note, this isn't the same theory as our earlier discussion about managing your expectations. Lowering your expectations refers to avoiding an equal partner and consciously choosing someone below the level in which you see yourself. This sounds elitist because it is. Unfortunately, even today, social hierarchy still exists. When many dating app users decide to swipe right on an app, there is the implication that this person is on the same plane as them.

Kevin was out at a party, and he saw a girl, Donna, who was gorgeous and appeared to have a lot of money. He wanted to approach her, but his friends said, "She's out of your league, man."

Conversely, Kerry, a friend of Kevin's, was intelligent and funny, plus she had been in love with Kevin since the second grade. She even told him so last time they drank at their local hangout. Kevin didn't feel a romantic attraction, but he loved Kerry as a friend.

Kevin said to his buddy, beer in hand, "I'm going to talk to Donna. Just getting up the nerve."

"No offense, but she's out of your league, and you are setting yourself up for being smacked down," Kevin's close friend replied. "Dude, Kerry's been in love with you since like the fourth grade. It's always better to be with someone who loves you more than you love them. At least, that is what my mother says."

What would you have done if you were Kevin?

When I hear others proclaim that settling or dating below them is the way to go, it says more about the person doing it than the person it's done to. For example, if a woman or man wants to date someone who makes less than them, it's usually about power or their need for control. If a man or woman wants to date someone who is not as attractive, it could say much about their fear of abandonment. It comes down to an individual compensating for their relationship fears when they purposely date "down."

And what about the saying that it's best to be with someone who loves you more than you love them, as in the example with Kevin above. Again, it says more to me about the individual settling than the one perceived to be more in love. Do you want a relationship built on addressing your fears or instead, mutual respect and equal love for one another?

Takeaway: You stand in line and proudly declare your coffee selection, "I'll have a tall, caramel Frappuccino, blended, with soy milk, and a dash of chocolate powder." What if you could be as decisive in choosing a partner, "I'll have a nice guy, who appreciates the importance of family, wants kids of his own, and likes long walks on the beach?" How much easier would that be, right? Well, it can be that easy. Look for someone who shares your core values in life while challenging you to be the best version of yourself. Age and social status shouldn't come into play, ever.

"Love at first sight is possible, but it pays to take a second look." - Unknown

Each of the myths we talked about in this chapter arises when people search for someone special to add to their lives. Although friends and family can be well-meaning at this time, you must set your boundaries around how much advice you will take in. As we stated in chapter one, consider the advice giver's motives—filtering the direction is critical. So, if you are trying to find that special someone:

- Create reasonable and realistic expectations for yourself and your future partner and identify those core values you want your partner to have.
- Dating is about opening yourself up. It is a time to be vulnerable, patient, and kind to yourself.
- Think about your advice-giver's motives and factor that into the weight you give their comments.
- And remember, if you can't love yourself, then you can't effectively love another.

We've just gotten started debunking the myths around relationships. Let's keep going to make your love life more fulfilling and significantly less complicated!

CHAPTER 3 –
DATING TO RELATIONSHIP?

Imagine the following actual scenarios:

- A man goes to the bank every day for the past ten years, and one day, a new teller shows up to take his deposit—instant connection. He asks her out before the transaction is done. She says yes. They have been married for over forty years.
- A woman walks her dog the same route and passes the same people each day. She gets sick and asks a friend to come to walk her dog. She resumes her walks a week later. As she comes upon a fellow dog walk- er, he says hi and walks past—just like always. Then from behind, he calls out, "You feeling better?" They both turn and share a smile—an instant connection. The two have been together for over 20 years.
- High school sweethearts separated for college and pursued careers, marriages, children, and sadly divorces. Thirty years later, they meet by chance on the main street of their hometown. They spend the next thirty years together, wondering why they let each other go.

Some refer to the above situations as examples of magical sparks that flew be- tween two lovers destined to be together forever. Isn't that the ideal scenario based on every movie out there? That one day you will wake up, walk out your front door, and there he is, waiting for you on a white horse, holding a bouquet of red roses, and suddenly you know he's your true love? Cue the sound of screeching brakes!

I am always honest to a fault with my patients, and I plan on giving you noth- ing less in this book. The above stories are heartwarming and romantic. Yet, I envision many of you glancing over at your partner after reading them and wondering, *Is the person beside me, watching television, and picking his teeth, the one? Did we ever have that moment, and maybe I missed it?*

I can't answer those questions for you. What I can tell you is romantic connections are not the result of some unexplained chemical reaction. Individuals don't just meet because of some cosmic pull and suddenly realize they've found their one true love. It doesn't work that way. Again, it makes for good material for romance novels and movies only.

Attraction, however, is natural and, scientifically speaking, the reason people come together. But there is more to interest than just how you may find someone physically appealing. There are other components when we feel something for someone: proximity, similarity, and reciprocal attraction. All these components will impact our feelings of "chemistry," "magic," or "sparks" that many describe when you fall for someone.

We tend to fall for people close to us. And by close, I don't mean your next-door neighbor who mows his lawn while exposing his beer belly or the guy in the office next to yours, who belches all day. Instead, I am referring to physical or emotional closeness. For example, if the person you like is traveling for the next six months, but you talk or text multiple times a day, intimacy is established. Conversely, if you have a partner who lives in the same house, but you rarely talk or do things together, that could be perceived as distant.

Similarity is another factor of attraction. Science supports the premise that individuals bond with others who share similar beliefs and values—we discussed this at length in a previous chapter. And scientifically, it has also been proven that people feel attracted to someone who is attracted to them. This is not suggesting that you wrap your arms around the person you like and declare your love to get them to say, "I love you too!" It doesn't work that way. It just means if someone finds you attractive, it increases the likelihood that you might feel the same.

When you take all these components and put them in play, someone *may* experience a moment or a feeling that drives the theory of chemistry, magic, or sparks flying. But now you know the truth. It's not chemical. You didn't get bitten by some love bug or hit with cupid's arrow. It was the power of attraction. And it most likely will happen more than one time in your life.

But what happens after the initial attraction? Why is it that many people can score a date easily but can't turn those so-called intense connections or initial sparks into something more lasting or meaningful?

I had a patient come into my office, Ami, who showed up in tears. As a therapist, this is not an uncommon thing. I sat her down, handed her a box of tissues, and waited for her to compose herself.

"I'm sorry," Ami said, sniffing and choking back her tears.

"Don't apologize. When you're ready, you can share with me why you're so upset."

Ami blew her nose loudly for her petite 4'11" frame. "I'm ready."

"Ok, so what happened that made you so upset?"

"I think I found the perfect guy for me."

Not the answer I was expecting, I tilted my head, signaling my confusion, and waited for her to finish.

"We had a moment over the deli counter when he looked at me and asked me if I wanted a sandwich. I said yes, and then the next thing I knew, I handed him my phone number."

"Ok, and?"

"We went out on a date. And you know I've had a lot of dates lately."

I shook my head in agreement. Ami was a serial dater.

"But it was magic with him. He was different. He's the one. I told him I wanted to bring him to meet my parents. I was so sure. I haven't heard from him since. I know it's taboo to do that, but I did, and now I lost my one true love."

Ami resembled a girl on the previous night's episode of *The Bachelor*, and I wondered why people are so convinced initial attraction means far more than it does? Did Ami lose her one true love? No. But did she make some incorrect assumptions? Well, let's find out that answer as we debunk some critical myths around dating after that first moment of connection.

"Love is a fire, but whether it is going to warm your hearth or burn down your house, you cannot tell." - *Joan Crawford*

Myth #7: Soulmates exist

In the movie *Shrek*, classic Disney, Fiona twirls around in front of Shrek, stops and clasps her hands in front of her heart, and declares she is ready for a kiss from her one true love. As I've said before, life is not a Disney movie. There may be one person for you or many. No one knows what life holds for them, but we create unrealistic expectations when we think in terms of fairy tales.

In the movie *Good Will Hunting*, Robin Williams defines a soulmate as "Someone who challenges you. Someone who touches your soul." I like this definition for its content and because it challenges the theory that there is only one lid for your pot. Let me explain. Do you think there could be more than one person for you who could fit Williams' definition? Yes, absolutely. We can connect with more than just one person who can fulfill our emotional and physical needs. Yet, some are lucky enough to find one person and stay with them for their life; for others, they find individuals who work for a time in their lives.

Takeaway: The movie *Cinderella* would have you believe only one foot could fit the glass slipper. Ah, not sure that makes sense. Suppose Cinderella was a size 6, was she the only size 6 in the whole kingdom? Hardly. So, do you think there is only one person who is specifically meant for you? We all hope the person we are with will last forever. It's something to work towards, but life is unknown. Be open, honest, and realistic, and you will find someone who challenges you and touches your soul for life or maybe for now.

Myth #8: Don't broach serious topics too early

Regarding my patient Ami, do you think she should have approached the topic of meeting her parents so soon? I think most of you would agree that bringing up something significant, like meeting one's parents, should not take place on the first or second date. Ami should have waited to see how this potential relationship unfolded. If they were compatible and wanted to take the following steps of bringing others into the relationship, they could proceed collectively.

Specific topics are taboo to bring up in the beginning. Now, I hesitate to make a list for you because, like most things, some are situational and dependent on the individuals involved. But my rule of thumb advice is to always keep the first few dates light and enjoyable. This is the time to get to know someone and be sure you're compatible, at least on the surface. It's also a time to find out if you have specific opposing values that may create troubles later or turn out to be flat-out deal-breakers.

For example, you go on a first date, and all the other person does is show you pictures of their car. It's a nice car, but you should ask yourself: Does this guy have more going on than just a love of his car? If not, can you connect if cars aren't your thing? This may be a deal-breaker. Conversely, if you find out that they also like long walks on the beach and Sunday night football as you do, then it might be a signal for a second date.

Once you get to know the person, you can judge when they may or may not be open to having deeper discussions. Again, on the first date, you want to find out basic information. Think of the first date as an application process: Are you an only child? Where were you born? What are your hobbies? On the second date, you will have basic knowledge of that person, so you can relax and perhaps let the conversation flow naturally into more profound subjects.

Typically, no matter who you go out with, they either love or hate talking about themselves. The person who talks freely about themselves will give you all the information you will need to assess if they are right for you. However, sometimes if they are excessively fixated on themselves, that may be a clue for you to run. But if you feel it's like pulling teeth to get personal information from your date, start looking for clues. Picking up signs is a great way to gain knowledge without an interrogation. Not everyone loves to talk about themselves.

For example, you take a walk along the water after a nice dinner. A family walking the other way is struggling with an unruly two-year-old. Your date turns to you and whispers, "Ugh, I would never let that happen with my child when I eventually have them." Bingo, now you know they eventually want a family. Pick up the clues and keep them in your pocket for deep, meaningful conversations as you progress toward a relationship.

Note the first few dates are also the time to keep your BS meter on full alert. Keep your eyes open for things that may not align with your core values or answers that are too perfect. Individuals may intentionally try to reel you in by being what they think you want. Or, if they avoid specific topics, that can also be a clue something is off.

Takeaway: Keep your first date conversations light and breezy like the clothing you wear on a hot day. This time is just exploratory. Like you would never see an archeologist use a backhoe in search of fossils', don't push too hard, too fast, or too soon. You could make that person run away faster than Usain Bolt. Use the soft, casual approach, look for clues in what they say, and let everything flow naturally.

Myth #9: Don't discuss exclusivity too early

I heard a story about Joy, who would meet her dates on dating apps quite easily. She was attractive, intelligent, financially independent, and men responded well, so she never had a shortage of prospects. Her friends wondered why she could never get past the first or second date. After some digging, they found out that Joy routinely asked her date's long-term intentions just after being served dessert. Most dodged the question and never asked her out again. Others gave her a second date but did not consider a third when she repeated the question.

This is where I caution many patients. A date or two should never be termed as a relationship. Control your need to attach yourself to anyone like a barnacle to a boat, no matter how over the moon you may feel for this person. Don't fall into the trap of thinking you found your soulmate, and from that moment on, you will be stuck like glue for all eternity. Calm yourself and your emotions down. Take a deep breath and take things slow. If you are meant to be together forever, it will happen. If not, rushing things won't help. You could end up scaring a good partner away.

Some patients have claimed, "Well, I just want to know now where things are going. I don't want to waste my time." I hear them. There is some truth about not wasting time on someone who will never want the same things. I recommend, if this is truly important to you and you don't want to waste a second with someone not looking for the same things as you, then it becomes more of *how* you approach the subject, than *if* you discuss it.

For example, you might start the conversation by saying, "I know this is soon to bring this up, but I am looking for "X," and I want to know if you are looking for the same thing." But if being forward is challenging for you, then look for clues within your conversations, as discussed in the previous myth. See how they talk about family or their careers and pick up on their inclinations. If they imply their career is their sole focus, you might assume that a committed relationship is not in the cards right now. But it's always best to be direct, rather than go on assumptions only.

Takeaway: Whether you go for the direct "don't waste time" approach or sit back and let things happen, it depends on you and what you're comfortable with. I always recommend being true to yourself and do what works best for you. But understand that forcing things will rarely work in your favor to get to that level of a committed relationship. A little patience, coupled with an open heart, will give any potential relationship a fighting chance.

Myth #10: Don't introduce them to friends and family

Meeting the family is a milestone in any relationship. Typically, it occurs in the earlier stages. Defining "earlier" and the appropriate time can be difficult; too early, it could be off-putting to your special someone, too late or not at all, could signal you're not serious. When a person chooses not to introduce you to family or friends, it's called pocketing and usually a red flag.

Pocketing is more than avoiding the awkward meeting with the parents. This person your dating will avoid or hesitate about introducing you to their friends or family or other people they know either through social media or in person. Basically, they keep you in their pocket and hide you from their world—never a good sign.

If you feel like you are a secret, then time to figure out why. There may be a good reason as to why, but either way, you must address it. The best approach is to ask their intentions. Then express your desire to meet their friends and family. If this is a situation that they are hiding something, such as a spouse, then better you know now. If they are perhaps fearful you would judge them based on their family or friends, you can talk things through. Provided you both see the relationship heading in the same direction, you can develop a plan to meet their family or friends when it works for each of you.

Takeaway: Timing is everything. When you have a strong connection with someone romantically, there is often a rush to take things to the next level. The desire to gain a more profound attachment by knowing the other person's family and friends can be intoxicating. Slow it down. Ensure you and the person you are dating are of one mind about moving forward, then discuss when the timing will be correct. Give yourself, the person you're dating, and the relationship, time to form before bringing others in.

Myth #11: Always look perfect

This myth always reminds me of the Kardashians. The entire cast is perfect, from clothing to makeup, to nails, to Botox lips, and so on. Yes, they are entertaining to watch, but the subliminal messaging can be troubling for some; the better you look, the better your life. Do I believe this? No. Do I think others absorb this message subconsciously? Yes. But I would ask: What happens when the person you are dating sees the real you? How has it worked out for the Kardashians to search for the right man? Not well, if you follow them.

At the beginning of this chapter, we talked about attractiveness and the layers or elements that make it up. The first layer is the physical. So, I liken the appearance to the gatekeeper or bouncer—it's the first level of defense, so to speak. I know people are taught that beauty shouldn't be the only factor, and it's not. But it can't be denied that initial judgments are based upon what we see in front of us, such as a person's looks. However, once you get to know someone on a deeper level, their other qualities will impact how you see their outward attributes. A good-looking guy can become gorgeous if their personality is appealing to you. A gorgeous-looking girl can become ugly if she has a horrible attitude.

Therefore, looks do matter but only to a degree. It may sound shallow, but it's a starting point, not an end-all point; it ignites a spark, but it won't keep the fire burning. Kanye West was married to Kim Kardashian. Kanye was known to dictate Kim's look at every turn, from her trainers to outfits. That level of interest in the physical could be considered over-the-top and something I would caution anyone to look deeper into. And clearly, it didn't have a positive effect for those two since they are now divorced. So, in your life, keep your eyes and mind open. You don't want someone who is focused solely on your physical appearance.

On the flip side, your outward appearance can also be indicative of your inward appearance. Suppose you are a person who takes care of yourself by eating right and exercising regularly. In that case, you are more likely to have higher self-esteem. The higher your self-esteem, the more comfortable you will be with yourself, which is attractive to others.

Takeaway: Have you ever walked into a store and been immediately attracted to something on display, but after further inspection, your opinion changed? Well, the same thing is true in the search for love. What we see in front of us is the start, but not the end.

You should, however, try and look your best for yourself, not solely to attract someone else. If you focus on feeling good for yourself, you will eventually attract a person that fits you.

Myth #12: Never trust anyone who sleeps with you right away

Have you ever watched the Millionaire Matchmaker? The host, Patti Stranger, always utters the words, "Why buy the milk when you can get the cow for free." It's an old saying that has no place in modern society. Yes, the stigma still floats around out there, but it's a dying myth. To prove it, let's look at some statistics:

- In a study in 2013 where 1,000, 18- to 35-year-olds were polled, 83% of women believed sex on the first date would make the man lose respect for them. While 67% of the men said they would not lose respect for a woman if she had sex with them on the first date (Wilser, 2013).
- In 2017, Match did a study where they found that men were 3x more likely to use a one-night stand to start a relationship (2017).
- In 2016, a Singles in America study revealed that 25% of men started a long-term relationship from a one-night stand (2017).
- According to the Singles in America study, 48% of singles are likely to sleep with someone if there is a connection (2017).

Have I made my point? It looks like the sexist double-standard is turning. Women, like men, should decide between the pursuit of something physical early on in the relationship. It all comes down to what works for the individuals involved.

Empowerment aside, some experts warn against moving too quickly to the bedroom. Scientifically speaking, women are flooded with oxytocin after sex which will cause them to emotionally bond with their partner. This is not the case with men. If things don't work out or, in fact, become the relationship the woman hopes for, the pain of being ghosted or ignored, or rejected by the man, can be intense.

Also, there is a theory that once sex is involved, it clouds a person's judgment. For example, suppose you meet a guy and from first sight are like a magnet to metal. You sleep together, and the sex is incredible. On the next date, he tells you he can't ever see himself getting married or having kids. Although this news would have been a deal-breaker previously, now you're attached. You let his comment slide for now. You convince yourself he may change his mind. Guess what? You've just compromised your wants and needs while potentially wasting your time. Nothing good could come from this.

Takeaway: A positive first date can allow for a level of excitement that can cause even the most conservative individual to lose some inhibitions. I'm all for being open to the potential for love. But just like a sign might read on a dangerous road, "proceed with caution," keep your eyes open to avoid potential problems.

Myth #13: Don't call for x number of days

Kelly left the date feeling like this could be it. She was everything he desired, beautiful inside and out, sweet but edgy, and best of all, she made him laugh. He got home, threw himself on the bed as he replayed every minute of the date in his head. Sitting up, he grabbed his phone and immediately dialed her number. No answer, so he dials again. Cue the screeching brakes again!

Ok, the date went well, and you're excited. I get that. But whether you did the deed on the first night, got swept up in the initial attraction, or you could see yourself with this person for the long haul, pull back on the reigns and slow that run-away horse. Do not start calling the minute you left the person, and if they don't pick up, push the redial. This stalker mentality sends the "I'm needy signal" and can be extremely off-putting. It is certainly acceptable to call the day after, but no longer than a week. If you call the next day, it's sweet. If you call a week later, the person has already assumed you moved on or, worse, forgotten about you.

Now suppose you just exchanged numbers with someone you met. You two had a great connection, and you both felt it. Do you call them right away? Do you text them right away? Again, I will give you the same advice as before: a day after is good, but no longer than a week.

Takeaway: How many times did your parents tell you to have patience growing up? When you had to have that new bike or the latest toy that all your friends had, did you get it instantaneously? No. Because your parents were preparing you for life—nothing worthwhile comes easily or for free. And in relationships, whether they are on fire or imploding, you need to be patient. Timing is everything, and just like you must wait for the things you want in life, you have to give your potential partner time and space—not too much and not too little—it's a balancing act.

In the example of Ami, she may have approached the meeting of the family far too soon. But she got attached to the guy too quickly as well. When individuals meet someone they like, that butterflies-in-the-stomach-emotion can make the mundane day-to-day exciting. I get it. Enjoy it. I'm not saying to be all business without feelings. Feel with an open mind and take your time to move to the next level. Be sure the object of your desire feels the same way and proceed down the bumpy road of relationships with caution.

"Some people are worth melting for." - Olaf

Some people claim that when you find the right one for you, you will just know it. And while that may be true for some, it's not valid for all. In life and love, patience is critical. Once you meet someone, take your time to determine if you are a good match. Combat the rush of emotions telling you to sprint to the finish line and declare your search over by changing your Facebook status.

Make those initial interactions work for you. Collect all the information you can about this new person and make *informed* decisions. But most importantly, if you think or feel this could be the one, give yourself time. Time will either validate those feelings or negate them. And although falling in love is all about how we feel about someone, it should also be done over sufficient time with our eyes open to the facts.

CHAPTER 4 –
NEW RELATIONSHIP

Joe was the roommate of Meg's high school friend, Connor, when they met. They hit it off right away, sharing a love of friends, family, hiking, and reading John Grisham novels. From their initial meeting, the two were inseparable. And eight months later, at the annual family Fourth of July barbeque, filled with family and friends, Meg brought Joe in to meet everyone.

Joe's nerves got the better of him, and he downed a few beers to lighten himself up a bit. And as he tossed one beer in the recycling can, Meg took his hand and led him over to a group of about six adults having an intense discussion. Meg proudly introduced Joe as her boyfriend.

"So, Joe, nice to meet you. Maybe you can settle an argument a few of us are having with our wives here," said Alex, a self-impressed bond trader, who liked to put on a show for everyone.

"Sure," Joe jumped at the chance to connect. He turned and smiled at Meg, who shifted her stance, a little uncomfortable with what these guys would ask. They were notorious for debating subjects to death, being judgmental, and putting others on the spot. She looked over her shoulder, as her mom raised a glass of sangria toward her, a sign of support.

"Well, we've all had our share of car accidents, but the women here outweigh us. We guys think the ladies need to accept that we're better drivers. What do you think? Are you better than Meg here?" Alex prompted, pointing his drink in Meg's direction.

Still loose from his beers, Joe quickly responded, "A blind beaver is a better driver than Meg." He burst out laughing. "She nearly took out a light pole this past week, and the week before that, she got pulled over for running a red light."

Dead silence. Meg squeezed his hand, but Joe continued unphased. "And Meg asks the cop, 'No one was coming, why did I need to stop?'" Joe cracked himself up.

The other couples nervously chuckled as Meg pulled Joe away, saying, "We have to go help Dad with the burgers."

"Why did you pull me away? That's a funny story!"

Meg, slightly annoyed, quipped, "Yes, it's funny, but for anyone other than the people I'm working for this summer. I'm supposed to drive their kids to different day camps next week!"

There is nothing like the beginning stages of a relationship and making those first introductions, blending the old with the new. This euphoric stage can cause you to let your guard down and think everyone you love will love this person too, that no rain will fall on your parade, and that your feelings for this person will conquer all. Truth be told, this phase will pass.

I'm not trying to be a Debbie Downer. I love this phase in a relationship because you are past the stressful dating stage and seeing yourself as a couple, but without any baggage yet. And I say yet, because as much as I love romance, I am a realist. I want you to have this phase and enjoy it, but be open-minded to the pitfalls and potential derailing advice and actions that could send you back to the dating apps.

"All you need is love. But a little chocolate now and then doesn't hurt." – Charles M. Shultz

Myth #14: Always trust your family and friends when it comes to your relationship

If you're breathing, then you've heard of the show, *The Bachelor*. For those of you who don't watch it but know the premise, what you may not be aware of is that toward the end of the season, the bachelor takes two girls to meet his family. What could go wrong there, right? Could you imagine parading two different people in front of your parents to get their opinions on which one they think is best for you? Nightmare!

And even if you are not a fan, you may have heard of the 24th season with a bachelor named Peter Weber. Peter's mom Barb was a standout with her overly dramatic reaction to the two girls her beloved Peter brought home. Talk about mommy issues! The two girls, Hannah Ann and Maddi, were quite different. Maddi planned to remain a virgin until marriage, and well, that ship had sailed for Hannah Ann. However, it was clear to the viewers that Peter had significantly greater affection for Maddi, regardless of Barb's awkward obsession with Hannah Ann.

Barb, an obvious helicopter mom, felt she knew Peter better and that Hannah Ann would be the right one for him. Cue the tears and emotional breakdown of Barb's full-on blitz to force her son to choose the girl she wanted for him. In the end, Peter went with his mother's choice, but sadly and not so shockingly, it didn't last. Does anyone else think Peter needs to set some boundaries with Mom?

So, what's the point of this story? You have this new person in your life, and your excitement is driving your need to share them with those you love—family and friends. But, as life sometimes does, the actual meeting doesn't always go as well as you imagine it. We saw this with Megan and Joe at the beginning of this chapter. Whatever the scenario, take a breath and accept it for what it is, an awkward time.

Often, I have patients share disastrous stories of when they introduced their significant other to family or friends. Their mother pushed too hard with questions, or their best friend passed harsh judgments. Either way, they ended up getting too much unwanted positive or negative advice such as:

- Don't put all your eggs in one basket.
- You can do better.
- You should get married.

Whether your family or friends start planning your beachside nuptials or they have decided this person should be sent packing, you need to take a breather. I am not saying don't listen. I am telling you to calmly evaluate the motives of the person giving you the advice.

For example, your friend Marsha says you shouldn't put all your eggs in one basket. What is she telling you? She is giving you the advice to not hitch your trailer to his car. Don't stop looking for the right person because this guy is not it. Take a breather, don't get defensive, and thank Marsha for her advice. Then, when you are alone and calm, frame the situation: What is Marsha's story? What are Marsha's motives?

I know we've discussed listening to family and friend's advice in a previous chapter. My direction here is the same. Most individuals advise others for selfish reasons. They may think they are doing it for your benefit, but the advice serves them quite often. Perhaps, Marsha is that friend that's eternally single because no one fits her idea of perfection. In this instance, you could assume her advice is coming more from her need to make herself feel better and have you join her high-expectation approach. Throw her guidance in the trash and follow the facts about your love based on what you know.

But what about the flip side? What about those family and friends that already have your wedding speech written? This can add pressure to a new relationship. Again, stop and think about what's driving this advice. Is it from someone who just wants to see you married for selfish reasons or someone who objectively likes this person and sees them as a good fit for you? Either way, thank them for their opinion. Set boundaries around your relationship, instead of being rushed, saying, "Thank you for the love and support. I am so happy you like them. But we're taking it slow and would appreciate it if you could give us this time to get to know one another before adding marriage pressure."

Takeaway: Introducing a partner to friends and family can be like a game of dodgeball. Just think of you and your partner standing on one side while both of your friends and family hurl advice and opinions at you with marked intensity and speed. There will be much bobbing and weaving, but if you are adept at seeing where the balls are coming from, you will be successful in staying the course.

Just as they tell you to stop, drop, and roll, when you are on fire, I will ask you to stop, breathe, and examine motives when you're hit with others' unwanted opinions. Understand that people will often say they give you advice because they love you. But more times than not, they dish out their opinions for their benefit, not yours. When you decide, based on fact, not the desires of your loved ones, like bachelor Peter did, you will establish boundaries and make the choices best for you.

Myth #15: You have the right to read their messages

"Do you know what the asshole did this time?" My patient Lexi asked, as she threw her hands up in the air and slammed them down on the couch, and glared at Max, her boyfriend, sitting at the other end. You could drive a truck between the middle of these two individuals.

"Lexi, why don't you tell me what happened," my eyes darting to the clock as I had a feeling this would take a while.

"He's been acting weird lately."

"You're crazy!" Max shouts.

I put my hand out to let them know to take it down a notch. I could just imagine the waiting room's reaction to all their screaming, "Max, let Lexi explain herself first."

"Well, he was acting weird like I said," Lexi snapped in Max's direction, "So, when I came home and saw his phone on the counter and saw the bathroom door was shut, I looked at his messages."

"She doesn't have the right to read my texts!"

"Max, let her finish, please," I say in a calm voice, like a preschool teacher addressing a four-year-old.

"We're in a relationship, and we should share everything! Yes, I read a text he hadn't sent, and I flipped out. I mean, he asked for a nude selfie! I deleted it and just went—"

"Nuts! You went nuts! If you'd looked, you'd have seen the text was for you! But no, you went nuts, and now we're here with the crazy-head-fixer lady!"

"Ok, I'm a therapist, and I think we can sort this all out."

Then, Lexi turned on a dime. She melted like a snow-cone in July, "It was for me?"

Who's right and who's wrong? A study shows that 34% of women and 62% of men snoop on their partner (Curtis, 2013). Frequently, the reasons people cross the line and look at the other's texts or emails have more to do with the person doing the sneaking than the person being sneaked on. Motives of the snooper can be jealousy, feelings of inadequacy, fear of loss, or worse, they are guilty of the act they are looking to catch the other doing.

We will talk a little more about some of these motives later in this chapter. Still, the real question is: Is invading your partner's privacy within your right if you're in a relationship? Well, that depends on the individuals involved. I know some couples who are all about an open-door policy, right down to using the bathroom. At the same time, others don't share things they consider too personal. The problem comes into play when, like Max and Lexi, the two can't agree on boundaries.

If you can discuss the issue and agree on what's on or off limits, you can move forward with mutual respect. But disagreeing and snooping anyway, despite your mates' feelings, isn't appropriate or demonstrative of the trust you are trying to build.

Takeaway: Trust is the basis for a healthy relationship. If you fail to trust one another, ask yourself, "Why am I still with this person?" With anything in life, we bring into it some amount of baggage from previous experiences. If you've been lied to, you might lean toward knowing everything about your current partner—your scars dictate it. Or, if you've felt overly controlled in the past, you may be ultra-protective of your privacy. No matter the cause, it all comes down to communicating with your current partner and sharing your feelings.

Myth #16: Lie when it comes to how many people you've slept with

Telling someone the number of your sexual partners should not be on the top of your to-do list. Let's face it, it's never a fun conversation, no matter which end you're on. No one wants to hear that their boyfriend or girlfriend had a ton of experience before them, and no one wants to share their past escapades—after all, it's in the past. Best to let sleeping dogs lie, they say, or is it?

We like to brag about many things in life: I got a promotion, got a new car, bought five new outfits for our trip to Mexico, and so on. But no one wants to stand up and say, "I've slept with just about everyone in this room!" However, there are definitive times when your past should be disclosed:

- If the person or persons you've slept with are still within you and your partner's social group or family.

- If you've slept with many individuals and you didn't always use protection.

Both of these instances could be a relationship deal-breaker if discovered at another time. Don't leave that information locked up, hoping it never gets out. That's like lighting a firecracker and hoping it never goes off.

I've heard many stories of the bride or groom finding out, at their wedding, that their beloved slept with one of the bridesmaids, groomsmen, or a wedding guest. This typically is followed by hurt and resentment, if not immediate divorce. Indeed, this is no way to start a marriage or any relationship.

Takeaway: Discussing your prior sexual experiences is never a comfortable scenario, no matter how open and secure you feel with your current partner. And it's not a conversation that needs to be had, unless there is a risk to your relationship. If you haven't slept with anyone they know or you've protected yourself from sexually transmitted disease, then you're good to keep the past in the past.

Myth #17: Their jealousy means they love you

"How are things going?" Shari asked Tina, who kept twirling her drink with a straw and seemingly lost in thought.

"Ok, I guess."

"Well, just last week, you were over the moon happy about Terrance, and now you look miserable."

"I love him, but I've started to notice how jealous he gets, and it scares me."

"What do you mean?"

"Last night, my brother's friend called me. You know Tony?"

"Yeah, he's like your baby brother!"

"Exactly, and he needed help with an essay for his Econ class. So, I helped him like always, but when I got off the phone, Terrance questioned me like: "Who is this guy? Why does he have your number?" I finally said, "Wow, you need to go.""

"And?"

"He left, all angry. But then this morning, he called and apologized and said, "I only get jealous because I love you, baby." He was so sweet, but something about it creeps me out.

"That's not a good sign, Tina. And jealousy is not a positive trait in anyone!"

As a therapist, I've heard many conversations like the one above. It's not uncommon for one person in the relationship to become jealous. Again, jealousy is more about the person feeling it than the person receiving it. The quote, "There is more self-love than love in jealousy," by Francois Duc de La Rochefoucauld, is so true.

In my practice, jealousy is a repetitive topic. I have patients who say, "Well, I'm jealous, so doesn't that prove I love so-and-so!" And I am not the only therapist who has heard these words, "I guess I will marry him. After all, he gets so jealous that sometimes he slaps me around, so it must be real love." My response is always along the lines of, "No, my understanding of jealousy is that it does not prove love. It proves insecurity."

I fear for anyone who thinks physical or emotional abuse is out of love. Although there are degrees or levels of jealousy, it doesn't come from love. Jealousy stems from fear or insecurity. The jealous person often feels like they might lose their partner or aren't good enough for their partner. It's never because they have such a strong affection for someone. The foundation of any relationship should be built on trust and respect. Jealousy is the opposite of trust and respect.

All too often, jealousy gets out of control and turns deadly. You don't want that for anyone, so if you see it, encourage the victims to get individual counseling. You may just save their life. This is especially true for teens and young adults. When immaturity mixes with jealousy, it can be a dangerous combination.

Takeaway: Just as binge eating has nothing to do with hunger, jealousy has nothing to do with love. No matter how flattered you may feel or what your partner tells you, jealousy is a red flag waving in your face. Stop and take notice. Have a calm, rational, adult conversation with your mate about how jealousy makes you feel, and try to get to the root of the problem. If your partner doesn't respect your privacy and stops trusting you, you need to open your eyes to the issue and make some tough decisions.

Myth #18: Love is all you need

Do you think John, Paul, George, and Ringo were right? Did The Beatles hit single tell us all we need to know? Is love all you need? Well, it's a start, but certainly not all. Ask anyone who's been through a break-up, and they will tell you that's all a bunch of hogwash, as the Brits would say.

What do I mean? Well, just because you love someone doesn't mean you can get through any difficulty. What brings you through tricky times is your ability to work together toward a common goal. If you disagree on the approach or the goal and are unwilling to compromise, well, then you will be stuck like a stick in the mud with no way of getting out.

Did you ever see the movie *The Bodyguard*, with Kevin Costner and Whitney Houston? Costner's and Houston's characters fall in love while he's her bodyguard, hence the title. But in the end, love wasn't enough because that emotion was all that they shared. Their values and their aspirations were utterly different. Hence, the lead track from the movie, "I Will Always Love You," plays as they go their separate ways.

Country singer Morgan Wallen released a song titled "More than My Hometown." The song's premise is about a guy saying goodbye to his girlfriend, whom he loved more than most things, but not more than he loved living in his hometown. He was unwilling to give up something that meant so much to him, even for love.

This is not to say all is lost if you fall in love and you aren't as compatible as you'd hoped you would be. If both individuals are willing to be open and put in some effort, love is a great place to start. These couples can begin by using visualization techniques, seeing themselves, their partner, and the relationship itself as the three parts of a whole. All three need to be nurtured with love, flexibility, openness, self-awareness, and emotional insight for growth and sustainability.

Takeaway: Just as you can't build a foundation on quicksand, you can't make a relationship where you're so far apart on the critical stuff you're unwilling to grow together. Love is vital but so too are the more practical elements. Passion alone won't support a healthy, long-term relationship.

*"I want someone who will look at me the same way
I look at chocolate cake."* - Anonymous

Enjoy this euphoric stage of your relationship. It's a time when everything is fresh and new, like an outfit you just took the tags off or sheets just out of the package. But you will experience difficulties, that is guaranteed. No relationship is immune. So, go forward with your eyes and heart open—set boundaries with family, friends, and your partner. Have meaningful conversations about what does and doesn't work for you. The only way to build any healthy relationship is to set some rules, communicate, build that trust over time, and be willing to do some work.

Chapter 5 –
Time To Get Serious

Kelsey strolls out of the bathroom wrapped only in a towel as Kyle lays in bed gazing at the television. "Hey, girl. Why don't you come over here, and I'll help you dry off."

Kelsey gives her best coy smile, "I'd love to, but I'm late for work. Raincheck?"

"You got it. I'll go make us some coffee." Kyle jumps off the bed and hugs Kelsey, and then draws her in for a long kiss.

"You make this hard," Kelsey whispers.

"Right back at ya."

"Gross," Kelsey laughs as they separate.

Ten minutes later, Kyle appears in the bathroom, a steaming cup of coffee in each hand, while Kelsey is applying her make-up.

"Here you go, babe."

She smiles, thinking, *this should be our every morning.* But as she looks in her makeup bag, she yells, "Crap!"

"What, you love coffee?"

"No, I forgot my foundation. I'm going to look like a connect-the-dots puzzle all day.

"You look beautiful to me," Kyle says, going in for a kiss, but he gets a hand to his face. He laughs and takes a sip from his cup.

"You know, Kyle, this would be a lot easier if you and I lived together."

Kyle chokes, and coffee shoots out his nose.

In my sessions with patients, I've been asked: "Why don't they see that moving in together is the next logical step?" Pump the brakes, people! You can't assume your definition of "the next step" is the same as your partner's. Defining what a deeper commitment means in a romantic relationship depends on the persons involved. One person may see getting serious as sharing their dessert, while another sees it as talking about marriage and kids. Also, once you've collectively defined your next step, it doesn't mean you will both be ready at the same time.

Kyle's choking on the coffee might have nothing to do with Kelsey's statement, or it could have everything to do with it. If Kyle and Kelsey haven't discussed the next step, then there is a chance they may not be thinking in the same terms and hence Kyle's physical reaction. Be sure you and your partner agree on what the next step is and when it should happen.

"Love can change a person the way a parent can change a baby–awkwardly, and often with a great deal of mess."
– Lemony Snicket

Myth #19: Living together will be a great way to "test the waters"

To live together or to not, that is the big question? Long gone are the stigma-inducing labels of "shacking up" or "living in sin." Since few individuals are waiting for marriage to have sex, there is little taboo around living together these days. But although the stigma has lifted, several myths still exist:

- You can test the waters.
- You can share costs and chores.
- You don't need a piece of paper to show your commitment.
- Living together will eventually lead to marriage.

What is "testing the waters?" Well, living together is a chance to simulate or play pretend to see if you can live together as a married couple. After all, we use this process with so many other things, like buying a car or sporting equipment. Taking a test drive or trying equipment out in a similar environment helps us see if that potential purchase will work. Will that car be fun to drive and bring me joy? Will this new golf club help me hit the ball farther? Before we plunk down a dime, we need to be reassured. The same must be valid for choosing a partner for life, right?

Before I give you a definitive answer, let's look at some basic statistics. Living together before marriage, statistically makes a marriage 50% more likely to end in divorce. Divorce rates among women, who live with their partner before marriage, are 80% higher than women that don't (Rosenfeld, 2018). And less than half of the people who move in together stay together for more than five years. So, do you think you know my answer now?

There are bizarre theories as to why divorce is higher among those that live together before the wedding. But I am more inclined to believe the idea of inertia, or what I call "the ties that bind" theory. No matter its name, this theory refers to the consistent and unrelenting pressure on the relationship from when two people start to live together. Like a vice-grip has two sides that come together to create a tighter force the closer they move together on an object, so too with couples who merge their worlds before marriage.

For example, individuals who move in together will often buy a dog, share expenses, possibly buy a home, and the ever-increasing activity of having children before making the union legal. With each "add-on," the wheel moves the vice just a little tighter, and the pressure intensifies, making it much harder to leave.

On a business trip with a few co-workers, I heard about a guy who'd been questioned if he planned to marry his long-time girlfriend. The man shrugged his shoulders, took a long sip of wine, and answered, "Well, I invested this much time. I guess I kind of have to." Wow, not a resounding over-the-top declaration of love. This story exemplifies that the longer a couple practices being married, the greater the chance they will stay together, but not necessarily because of undying love for one another. There is a theory that these individuals develop a greater sense of duty to the other person or develop a fear of having to "uncouple."

Ok, so testing the waters isn't necessarily a good reason, so what about sharing costs and chores. Again, I will revert to statistics. Statistics show that women in a cohabitating relationship contribute to more of the expenses. Statistics also show that women tend to do more of the household chores than men. Now, before you men start screaming about this passage, I didn't say all; I said *majority*. But as a therapist, what I can confirm, from the hundreds of couples that have come through my office, is that relationships are not a perfect equal split, either with money or chores.

What about the myth of not needing a "piece of paper?" What does a governmentally recognized union change? The answer depends on the mindset of the individuals involved. Typically, individuals that go by this myth are the marriage avoiders who have either been through a divorce themselves or have seen one first-hand. These individuals want the commitment without the legally binding agreement—they want a no-mess escape hatch that won't send them to the poor house. Again, not an excellent way to solidify a lifelong commitment. It's too easy to walk away and not have to do the work to keep things together. Just as we said in a previous chapter, any relationship will take work— no relationship is easy.

What about the theory that cohabitation is just a stepping-stone toward marriage? Well, that myth was truer in years past than it is today. In the 1970s, approximately 60% of couples that lived together got married. Today, that statistic has dropped to less than 40%. Although most still believe that living together will lead to a walk down the aisle and a stronger union, the statistics don't support it (Geiger, 2019).

Takeaway: I assume you can see that I am not a cheerleader for living together. It sets couples up to misrepresent what life will be like, adds unnecessary pressure too soon and puts women at a disadvantage emotionally and financially. This is a classic, look before you leap scenario. Keep things separate, at least until you know marriage is in the cards. Take your time to learn about the other person and yourself before becoming bound together in all aspects of life.

Myth #20: Each partner will do their fair share

When you move toward a committed relationship, some start to think of how they want the relationship. We've been told to set our boundaries early and establish rules from day one. So, I always laugh when I hear people declare they will have a true 50/50 partnership. A perfect 50/50 split lines up with perfection, and you know my opinion on expecting perfection. Generally, it would be easier to nail down Jell-o than to achieve a perfect division of responsibilities.

Forget romantic entanglements for a second. Do you only do your fair portion at work, or do you pick up the slack for others from time to time? How about growing up? Did you split chores perfectly with your siblings? That's what I thought! At times in life, you may do more than your fair share. This also means, at times, you may do less than your share. It's life, people. Nothing is a perfect 50/50 split.

Takeaway: As a kid, do you remember when you and your siblings argued over who got the last piece of cake? And how, when your mom told you to split it, you held those slivers next to each other, carefully examining them for equality? I think we can all relate to that, and yes, some still carry that mindset to their adult relationships. It's not a bad idea, just an unrealistic expectation. What do we do with unreal expectations? We reframe them. You can achieve an equitable split if you communicate needs, establish boundaries, and work together and accept that you may have more than your share with some things. Sometimes, close enough is as "perfect" as it gets. Again, employing Winnicott's theory (Myth #1) of "Good Enough" to sharing (2009).

Myth #21: Always communicate your needs

You're sitting on the couch and watching another movie on a Saturday night. Your man is snoring next to you. You roll your eyes because this is the third Saturday in a row you've done the same thing. You miss going out. You want and need to have some social interaction. What do you do? Do you lose it on him? Do you wake him and demand to go out that minute? Do you tell him how you feel and what your needs are?

I would say to communicate your wants and needs. But I would also tell you that it's just as important how you approach the conversation, as to having one at all. That is to say, do not start the conversation by snapping a picture of your man lying spread-eagle on the couch, snoring, and drooling, then post it on Instagram with the tagline, *Mr. excitement lights up another Saturday! #Yeahme.*

Your needs should be communicated between the two of you when you are both in the right mindset to have an open and honest conversation. We will discuss the art of sharing in the next chapter in more detail. Still, when you are in the beginning stages of a committed relationship, I suggest you account for two things when trying to get your message across:

- Know your audience.

- Be clear and unemotional.

When and how information is best received takes knowing your audience. If you are in a relationship and past the euphoric stage, you have started to see signs or been explicitly told when your partner is most open to receiving information from you. Know when, where, and how best to communicate, so your words can be received openly.

For example, I listened to a group of first responders talk to a new set of rookies right before entering the field. One of the young officers told a story about how, at the beginning of his career, he would work 24-hour shifts, and when he came home to his girlfriend the following day, she met him with a laundry list of to-dos for the day. He explained that he would have to drop his stuff and get right into what she had planned. Inevitably, he became irritable, and the two would exchange harsh words.

He finally said to her, "When I come through the door after a long night of running fire and EMS calls, I'm exhausted, physically and emotionally. I need an hour to regroup, and then I'm all yours. All I ask is that you give me that hour. Then, we can do whatever you want." The girlfriend wasn't hard on him. She didn't understand his needs. Once he explained it to her, she understood that their best communication would happen after he had that hour to rest his body and mind—fair request.

This fireman gave his girlfriend, now wife, some critical information. He set them up for success because now she knows when he's ready to receive information. And the fireman showed her that he wants to hear about her needs and take what she has to say seriously. It's a perfect example of setting a relationship up for better communication on those essential matters.

Next, know how to deliver information. Please don't post your grievances on social media or tell your friends. It will get back to your partner. You're an adult. Be clear about your needs and explain them calmly and maturely. Do not attack the other person in an accusatory way. Just plainly state what your needs are. If they love you, they should be able to understand your needs and work with you to make sure you're feeling fulfilled.

If, however, you are in any way afraid to talk to your partner because you fear they will have an emotional or physical reaction, then you need to re-think the relationship altogether. A mature, happy relationship is always in a constant state of adjusting for the people involved. Open and safe exchanges are critical for a solid future. Anything less is a red flag.

Takeaway: I'm not telling you something you don't already know how to do. You know when certain people receive information well and when they don't. You also know when you can deliver an unemotional conversation or when you are ready to rip someone's eyes out. Know yourself and know your partner. Communicate clearly, with your head, and without being overly emotional.

Myth #22: It's a good sign not to argue

People disagree and argue. Relationships are messy at times. No couple is immune. However, in this era of social media, individuals are compelled to promote their union as "trouble-free." Why? Because it makes them feel secure—they've bought into this myth. They post to Instagram and Facebook to affirm their lives as successful and to make themselves feel good. It's not only self-serving to the person posting, but it's highly inaccurate.

For example, think about the "#blessed" text under every millennial's post. This seemingly innocuous word perpetuates the idea that the picture you're looking at is representative of one's entire life. Or, if they aren't posting a photo, there is the ever-annoying snapshot of texts between the couple. It's as if they want the world to see a sweet exchange and assume that this is the complete picture of how they communicate every second—the "we never argue" implication.

Stop the madness! You are smarter than this. Relationships aren't without their issues, and it shouldn't matter how someone else views your life. This myth is a lie!

For those of you in the early stages of a committed relationship, your arguments may be few and far between because things are still new, and you're each trying to figure the other one out. But anticipate there will be times when the two of you do not agree and be thankful for them.

Why thankful? When anyone claims they "never argue" with their partners, I always question its validity. And if it is true, how strong is the relationship? This can either be a lie or a sign of individuals simply going along to get along. A strong relationship allows for freedom to voice your opinion, and when you express yourself, you may be met with a different idea. These differences will challenge you and create an opportunity for growth. When you argue in a way that allows both sides to speak freely, and each side listens to the other, a positive outcome is likely.

Takeaway: In the first year of a newly constructed home, the house adjusts to the ground that it's built on. When you buy a brand-new house, most builders will tell you not to make any improvements for the first year because the house will move slightly. And if you've ever lived in a newly constructed home, you will hear pops and cracks from time to time as the structure "settles."

A new relationship is no different. A new relationship is beautiful and shiny and something you want to show off. But that doesn't mean you are free of issues. Until you can "settle" down into a groove, you will have some movement or disagreements that will require fixing. It's healthy and to be expected. So, stop trying to live up to some standard set by others on social media!

If you allow yourself to believe the myth that not arguing is a sign of a strong relationship, then you are setting yourself up for failure and misery. Life is messy. Relationships are messy. Respectfully speak your mind, listen to your partner, and work to create a stronger union. It is that simple.

Myth #23: Your appearance doesn't matter once you're committed

Have you seen this new design theory of an open-concept bathroom? Yes, I am talking about a bathroom *in* your bedroom—exposed tub, shower, and yes, toilet. Sound appealing? Not so much, right? I had a conversation with a woman who said, "We still need some mystery in a relationship. We still need to put some effort into things to make ourselves desirable to the other person. I know I want my husband to put a little effort in." She made a strong argument.

We touched on this in myth number 11 regarding dating someone and needing to look perfect. I always encourage patients to think about their appearance in terms of what makes them feel good about themself. Do what makes you satisfied, and your inner and outer beauty will shine naturally.

Yet, consider the following caveat: Is your work complete once you are in a committed relationship? Think about it this way, if your partner works a physical job and comes home smelling ripe, are you necessarily ready to get busy in the bedroom? Not so much. Shower, people. Take care of yourself when it comes to basic hygiene. It's good for you, and it's suitable for your partner, so it will be right for your relationship.

Takeaway: As with so many things, there are levels to consider. Do you always need to look perfect, makeup done, and hair styled perfectly? Do you have to look like those Bravo reality stars who are in bed with full make-up? Do you need to dress in heels and sexy dresses to keep the fire burning? No, of course not. But some efforts, like running a brush through your hair, showering, shaving on occasion, are all excellent things to do with or without a romantic partner. Be yourself, but always try to be the best you can be, for yourself and your partner.

"You're like a dictionary - you add meaning to my life."
-Unknown

Newly committed relationships can be exciting and, at times, terrifying. You may want to jump into living together and play house because you are so over the moon in love with this person. But I caution you. Take your time to analyze what those big changes mean and if they will truly pay off for you, your partner, and your relationship in the end.

It's also crucial that you and your partner see each other as enhancements to each other's lives. You should never look at one another as replacements or the be-all-and-end-all of your existence. Don't stop making time for yourself, your family, and your friends. No matter how much you want to spend every waking moment with your love interest, you shouldn't. It's not healthy, and it's not fair to you, to them, or to the other individuals you love.

I always go back to that line from the movie, *The Help*, where the nanny, Aibileen Clark, says to the little girl, Mae Mobley, "You is kind. You is smart. You is important." Aibileen repeats this to Mae Mobley each day like a mantra. Although it may seem corny to do so, it's a good mantra to repeat to yourself when you're in a relationship. Relationships are lovely, but they can suck the life out of you too, if you aren't careful. You matter, and so does your partner—you are more than just what the two of you have together, a point that deserves repeating to yourself.

Chapter 6 - The M Word!

You could hear a pin drop as Walter stood up in front of the room with over 200 family and friends. His trembling hand reached into his breast pocket for the raggedy piece of paper. Unfolding the loose-leaf sheet, he drew a few chuckles from the group seated at the head table. The bride, Margie, nervously whispered to the groom, who seemed to gesture with his hand that it will be ok.

"Hmmm," Walter cleared his throat. "Um, ok," he fumbled with the mic being handed to him by the audio-visual tech guy. "You want to do the speech?"

The room let out a low roar of chuckles as the tech guy shook his head no.

"Ok, well, since he doesn't want to do it, I guess I will. As many of you know, like Mom and Dad over there, Jack is my older brother."

Laughter.

"Jack and I grew up sharing toys, clothes, and a bedroom until college, and now we share a house. Jack taught me to ride my bike, how to swim, bait a hook, and ski faster than Mom. Which, if you've seen Mom ski, it isn't that big of a feat, but I'll give it to him."

Laughter.

"To Jack's good, older brother, I was that pesky little brother who tagged along wanting to be just like him and his friends. I watched everything they did and tried to mimic it. I would always try to show off in front of them. Like one time, Jack let me join him and his friends skiing. I tried to make a move I saw on the X-Games." Walter points at his crooked nose, "I don't recommend it."

Laughter.

"But Jack never stopped me from tagging along. He took me everywhere with him and taught me about life. When he went to college, I would go up on weekends and visit. And even though I scored with more girls than he did, he never complained."

More laughter.

"Jack was ok to take a backseat to my attention-seeking ways. He always remained my steadfast protector. I love you, brother."

A collective "Ah."

Walter raised his glass, and the maid of honor stood, preparing to give her speech next. Margie let out a breath. Walter put his glass back down.

"You see, Jack was the perfect brother, roommate, and friend, then Margie showed up."

Silence.

"What can I say about Margie? Margie moved in with us shortly after she and Jack started dating, and well-" Walter looks to the sky, and every guest sucked in their breath, "Margie enters every room like her hair is on fire. I'm convinced she's got OCD and ADHD. She's like living with Martha Stewart on steroids."

Nervous laughter erupted.

"If you eat on the couch, she's waiting next to you with a Dust Buster. If you throw your socks on the floor, they will be washed, dried, and placed back in your drawer before you even notice them missing. And if you spend a little too long lingering with the fridge open, she closes the door on you and tells you to come back later."

More nervous laughter.

"But even though Margie can stress out a dead man, Margie has made Jack happier than he's ever been. Not to mention, she puts up with his pesky younger brother leaving his crap all over the house. And just last week, when my cheating girlfriend left me, Margie sat with me, blared Luke Combs, and helped me down an entire bottle of Jack's favorite whiskey. I'm blessed to have Jack as my older brother and now to have Margie as my annoying, but loving older sister."

A collective "Ah."

Just as Margie couldn't control her brother-in-law's words, you won't be able to control every inch of your marriage. There will be good points and bad points. There will be anger and laughter. There will be embarrassment and pride. But every positive or negative morsel of your marriage can be beautiful and celebrated—much like Walter's speech.

*"Marriage is hard enough without bringing
such low expectations into it."*
– Sleepless in Seattle, Walter (Bill Pullman)

Myth #24: Get hitched in your 20s for a long, happy marriage

Have you ever seen the TikTok videos where the guy drops to his knee, making the girl think a proposal is coming? And then wait for it, he doesn't propose, but asks her another question. A little cruel humor, yes, but what it shows is that society's desire for marriage is still present. However, the desire is not as strong it once was.

The percentage for Americans, ages 25 to 50, who never married, was around 35% in 2018. Go back to 1970 and that percentage is only 9%. And the median age of first-time marriages for women from 2014 to 2018 was 27.9, up from 2006 to 2010 when it was 26.3. For men, first-time marriages between 2014 to 2018, the median age was 29.7, up from 2006-2014 when the median age was 28.1. What do these statistics tell us? Fewer women and men are getting married, and when they get married, they're doing it later in life (Wang, 2020).

But despite those statistics, society continues to debate when the best time to get married is. The myth that a long and happy marriage requires you to marry young still floats around. And to the contrary, many believe getting married later is better for longevity. Let's examine these two schools of thought.

First, is the myth that getting married early is best. This theory suggests you and your partner will experience your twenties together without the demands of full-blown careers and a family's responsibilities. Spending copious amounts of free and fun times will allow you to grow and mature together to develop a strong relationship.

Second, there is the idea that if you prolong the time before you marry, you can pursue a career, the ability to achieve your personal goals, and enjoy the freedoms that come with being young and free. If you take this time for yourself, the theory extends to the thinking that you will "get it out of your system" and be less likely to feel like you missed out on things in your young adult years.

Both theories present interesting concepts, and I have done some reading to find out the perfect age to marry. But before you read about these studies, I caution you to relax. I don't want you throwing this book down in a panic and running out to find a partner because you are in a particular age range. Wait until you read my interpretation of these studies.

I recently read a study that suggested that the best time for an individual to get married is between 28 and 32 if you want to avoid getting divorced in the first five years. A sociologist out of the University of Utah, Nick Wolfinger, came up with the previous theory based upon data from 2006-2010 and 2011 to 2013 from the National Survey of family growth. Wolfinger wrote, "The odds of divorce decline as you age from your teenage years through your late twenties and early thirties. The chances of divorce go back up again through your late thirties and early forties" (Wolfinger, 2015).

Wolfinger stated the ages between 28 and 32 might be a good time to get married since most individuals have established careers at that point, they are better off financially, and they aren't so set in their ways. All of this makes this age range better suited to adapt to married life. But another researcher from the University of Maryland, Philip Cohen, using different data, said that the best age to get married to prevent divorce, occurs between 45-49 (Luscombe, 2015). Now, what do I think?

Statistics are just numbers, right? Yes and no. Statistical data can help us spot trends and make factual statements like 70% of women over the age of 40 don't shave daily, or 95% of men over 21 have had at least one beer, for example. Yet, when that factual data is used to make inferences, the lines blur between fact and supposition. For example, suppose someone reads the above data. And after reading the statistics, they state the following: Women over 40 let themselves go. And most men over 21 mostly drink beer. Those two statements are interpretations, not facts. Therefore, take the theories of Wolfinger and Cohen as exciting tidbits of information and nothing more. I don't want you running to find a partner in a mad rush before you turn 32 to prevent a divorce. Which, if you've read the prior chapters, you know I don't recommend rushing anything in the romance department.

However, data will support factual statements such as having money and a college degree reduces your chances of getting divorced. Getting engaged before living together also decreases your chances of getting divorced. So too, does waiting to have kids until after your nuptials. Statistical facts substantiate those statements, and you can take them to the bank.

Takeaway: If picking a life-long partner was as easy as picking an apple off a tree, life would be simpler. The problem is it isn't that easy. And when professors, researchers, or psychologists develop theories around when the "best time" to get married is, how does that help you? It doesn't. Who can predict when you find the right partner? And if you meet a possible love interest, who says you or they will be ready for a trip down the aisle by a particular age? There are too many factors at play. I can tell you for sure that it's more important to find the person you love than it is to worry about some arbitrary age that will supposedly give your marriage better odds. Honestly, if you want to know how to give your marriage better odds, read the rest of this book!

Myth #25: The secret to a happy marriage is to compromise

I'm going to say something that may blow your mind, but compromise is why so many marriages fail. Yes, I said why they *fail*. Not because they lack compromise, but because they have too much of it.

First, every individual is as unique as a snowflake. No two are exactly alike. No matter who you have a relationship with or marry, you will have disagreements. Second, because of differences, there will be conflict. This is a fact. You can't get away from it, can't avoid it. Third, honoring differences and learning about what is essential to each person enriches a relationship. It takes love to a deeper level.

So, if conflicts are inevitable, then why is compromising bad if it resolves an argument? To explain my position, let's look at how compromise is defined:

- To settle a dispute by mutual concession.
- Accept standards that are lower than desirable.

Does either of those definitions sound appealing to you? If you think back to your youth, how many times were you encouraged to compromise when arguing with another friend or sibling? Quite a bit, right? Ok, so you know what it means to have "mutual concession" or to lower your standards—basically giving up something to gain something. And as an adult, I can't see this concept being any more appealing than it was years ago. How can a compromise be avoided if you want peace in your home?

Let's look at a fictitious scenario: Mac and Reece are talking. Reece states that they were invited to join another couple for karaoke on Saturday. Mac says they can't go because they are going to his parents' for dinner. A perfect time for compromise? Ah, not so fast. Let's look at what happens from Reece's perspective:

Ah crap! He wants to go to his mother's for dinner to keep her happy. I'd rather gnaw my foot off than sit through another minute of listening to how she thinks I need to get a personal stylist to help me with my "bland" clothing choices. If I go, I will have to be insulted and take it because he will get mad if I say anything negative about his mother.

Now, let's see the way Mac is thinking:

Ah crap! The last thing I want to do is to go listen to her friends belt out another Britney Spears, "Hit Me Baby One More Time," while I sit there and contemplate hitting myself with a hammer, over and over. She'll be happy if I just go along because she loves hanging out with this couple, but I will hate it.

Ok, so now these two are facing each other and wondering: *Who will crack first?* Typically, at this point, compromise in marriage will happen one of two ways; either one person gives in to "keep the peace," or both give in. I hear some of you asking, "Isn't it the right thing to do for both of you, to compromise and give up something?" No, not for the long-term health of your union.

Let me explain using the above example. Here are how things should proceed, taking compromise out of the equation. Each spouse should ask the other *why* they want to do a particular thing. Find the truth, do not assume the other's reasons. Perhaps Reece wants to go out because she feels it will be a bonding time for them. Perhaps Reece then discovers that Mac isn't trying to appease his mom but has promised to help his dad with something. Once they know the truth behind each other's desires, they can come together and find a solution that is a win-win for both of them. By win-win, I am not referring to giving up something to get something. A win-win situation is where they both feel happy with the solution.

I had a patient who said his wife wanted to visit her parents like they do every year for vacation, except this year, he wanted to do something different. His wife was incredibly close to her family and would never want to do anything but visit them. However, I convinced him to express how he felt, to tell her what he wanted and why. My patient needed to explain his desire to spend some time alone as a couple and reconnect. They had demanding careers, and he felt they needed time alone. In the end, he and his wife had an open and honest discussion and came up with a solution that made them both happy. Again, it's not about one or both people sacrificing for the other, but about finding the win-win.

When conflicts arise, our first go-to is to assume the other person's position. As I just said, having an open conversation and putting aside incorrect or misleading assumptions rectifies the problem. Often, I have people complain they are always the ones making concessions because it's just easier to "go along." The adage of "go along to get along" or "peace at any price" can be a marriage killer.

If you find yourself in a position where you disagree with your partner, but you fear repercussions or anger if you go against it, this is serious. When one spouse tends to control through fear or intimidation, they force their wants on the other party. Often it can be the death of a marriage.

Takeaway: Just as decaffeinated coffee has no place in my coffee cup, selfishness has no place in a marriage. Any conflict or disagreement that arises should come from a place of "we," not "me." See what is best for both of you by mutually understanding what drives the other person's emotions. Once you stop assuming, then you can decide together what will make you both happy. If you don't do this, one or both of you will feel like they are constantly compromising. This feeling of always 'giving in' will build resentment between you and could derail your union.

Again, I would advise a couple when faced with conflict to do the following steps:

- Come to a calm place, stop assuming the other's reaction, and have an open discussion about what's driving their emotion behind the desire or need.
- Ask open-ended questions.
- Give the other time to respond and think through their answers. Often our partners must do some soul searching as to why they feel

the way they do.

- Then actively listen to their answers. One way to be sure you "heard" what your partner said is to repeat their responses back to them in your own words.
- Remember, you love each other and want the best for the other person, but also yourself. You both matter because you both make up the relationship.
- Come up with alternate solutions that make it a win-win for both of you.

Myth #26: Better communication is the key to wedded bliss

Cara put the magazine down and stared across the room at Josh as he flipped mindlessly through the channels. His legs spread out across the coffee table and his belly full of crumbs; her view looked bleak. He didn't seem open to conversation, but she had to give it a shot.

"Josh?"

"Hmmm," Josh muttered, eyes still fixed on the television.

"You want to try this communication game I just read about?"

He shifted his eyes toward Cara, completely suspect.

"Come on. It'll be fun!"

Josh let out an exasperated breath, "Ok, fine. Shoot."

"Well, we have to sit facing each other and look into each other's eyes while holding hands."

"Are you for real?"

Cara stood up and walked over to Josh and sat on the couch facing him. For all his grumbling, he did what she asked. "Ok, now what?"

"Well, we can talk about anything we want while looking into each other's eyes."

"I want to talk about how you make me do these stupid games you read about in those crazy magazines. And then, how you always get pissed off afterward. I don't get the point."

"Josh, be serious."

"I'm being serious."

"Ok, fine. Then let's talk about why I read all these magazines and ask you to do this stuff."

"I have no freaking idea, so you tell me."

"Because all you ever do is watch television, and we don't talk like we used to!"

"We're talking now!"

"I mean, really talk."

"Oh, I know, I talked to you last night. I asked for a little something, and you said no. See, we communicate!" Josh laughed at his attempt at a joke.

"Forget it!" Cara got up and left the room.

"See, I was right!" Josh yelled after her.

I have many experiences with patients who claim they've tried those magazine suggestions on how to communicate better with your partner, and it just ended up in an argument. Look, they are fun to read but rarely do they provide you with solid advice. It's like when you try to fix that dripping faucet by watching a YouTube video, and in the end, you call the plumber because your pipes are now spewing water everywhere.

When you first get married or before you get married, most don't experience a communication problem. Why is that? The answer is simple. You were connected then. The connection you have with your partner drives your ability to communicate. Your relationship is like plugging in your hairdryer. It won't work if you don't plug it in.

Let's look at this another way. Have you ever experienced a time when you felt disconnected from your partner? And then somehow the stars align, and you get some time alone, and it feels like old times again? Did you find yourselves sharing and bonding as you did at the beginning of your relationship? Did you wonder: *Why don't we do this more?* The answer is that our day-to-day lives can cause a disconnect. Individuals pour themselves into their careers, the kids, the house, and extended family, and the marriage often gets overlooked.

What am I telling you? To be a better communicator, make time for each other and get emotionally connected again. I'm not talking about booking a fabulous vacation you can't afford. I'm talking about carving out time to spend together each day, even if it's five more minutes in the morning hugging before you get up to rush to work. Or when you come home, grab a drink, turn off your phones, and talk about each other's day in the quietest, most relaxing place in your home. The point is to make time to connect. So, when you need to have those significant conversations, you will be more open to sharing and hearing one another.

Takeaway: I guarantee you're reading this and wondering why I am not promoting communication exercises or techniques? Let me ask you this, what is the difference between an organized youth sporting game and a group of kids in the backyard with no one refereeing them? In a backyard game, no one is manning the rules or checking to see if they are being followed correctly. And there are usually lots of arguments and debates about the rules. The same thing happens when couples try to use communication techniques by themselves.

Also, you did communicate before you got married. Do you think saying 'I do' has changed that? No. But there are additional stresses in life that may have come in between you both and caused an *emotional* separation. That distance can break those lines of communication.

The best way to get yourselves back on track emotionally is to ask yourself the following questions:

- Do I want to feel emotionally connected to my partner?
- Do I want to know how they feel?
- Are their feelings important to me, to us?
- Do I value and love my partner?

If you said yes to all of those questions, you are starting from a very good place. Now, all you have to do is make time to reestablish your connection. It doesn't have to be a spectacular gesture toward your partner. It can be as simple as bringing them their morning coffee and talking for ten minutes about anything before your day gets started. Or giving them a hug and a long kiss before they head off to their job. Make the collection of minutes in your day worth it, and you will be amazed how they will bring you back to communicating like you used to.

Myth #27: He or she will change once we are married

The waiter delivered two co-workers their lunch plates as the ladies talked business. They said thank you, and the waiter left them alone.

"No talking about work. We need a break!" Erica says, dissecting her sandwich, "I said no onions!"

"So, how are things going with the wedding planning?" Lisa asked Erica, before taking a bite.

"Ugh, I feel overwhelmed right now. I still have about ten things left to tackle before next week and no time to do them!"

"Isn't Carl helping?"

Erica let out a fake, dramatic laugh, "You're kidding, right? It's hunting season, silly. He is all about hanging with his hunting friends!"

"Well, you better get used to it, I guess," Lisa said, stabbing her salad with her fork.

Erica looked up, holding a sweet potato fry in one hand, using it as a pointer, "Oh, once we get married, he better change!"

Truthfully, many things will change after the wedding. Marriage is a considerable adjustment, even for those who lived together previously. Before marriage, you still held on to some sense of privacy or things that were just for you, like bank accounts or holidays with your family or your own home or apartment. After marriage, everything merges into one unit. It's living your entire life until your 20s on a side street. Then, when you find the right one and get engaged, you enter the onramp. When you marry, you merge onto the freeway. Yes, like Rascal Flats sang, "life is a highway!"

Marriage means you no longer just have to worry about number one. You have someone else to consider in all your decisions. You want to tell your boss to shove his job, but your spouse isn't bringing in enough to cover the mortgage by themselves. You want to see your parents on Christmas, but you have to consider now that your spouse may want to see their family too. You want to go away skiing all weekend with your buddies, but you and your spouse need to spend time together as a couple. There are so many new challenges and opportunities that come with marriage.

So yes, expect changes. But do not anticipate your spouse will suddenly morph into a more pleasing version of themselves or that they will give up their friends, family, or irritating pastimes. Cue the train horn! Marriage is not about loving a person for what they could be, but for who they are. Too many times, I've heard one person saying they hope the other will change once they get married. Should you find yourself uttering this expectation, then you are sowing the seeds of future resentment—a killer of emotional connection.

Conversely, if you're concerned your spouse will change after the ceremony, and you don't know if it will be good or bad, then this deserves an open and honest conversation. Understand, you are both going through a huge adjustment period. Still, if you can stay connected and keep the communication open, you will see the beautiful opportunities that come with marriage, such as sharing all of life's burdens and triumphs.

One area, many claim, will change after the wedding day is sex. I've heard many state that sex is something that you do before marriage because afterward is when sex stops. Although the frequency may indeed diminish, the openness and comfort between the two of you will grow, making the sex much more pleasurable for both of you. The more intimate your physical relationship is, the deeper your emotional ties and a much stronger marriage. Sex is a small part of a relationship, but it can become a big part of your disconnectedness if you don't have it.

Takeaway: Just as you should never buy clothing that is too small, with the anticipation that you will lose weight, you shouldn't enter into marriage hoping your partner will change. If you don't like something about them before marriage, then the time to communicate that is before you say, 'I do.' Talk through the issues and work it out before you start making the trek down the aisle.

Marriage is a significant change. You both will morph into a new sense of being, as a couple, and as individuals. But expecting that annoying habit to disappear because you are married is unrealistic and setting your union up for trouble. Talk it through. Anything that bothers you before you join together, will be there afterward.

Myth #28: Happy wife, happy life

Imagine you are out to dinner with a few other couples. Everyone is having a good time and talking about everyday struggles. Your wife compliments her friend, Tammy on her new necklace.

Tammy gushes, "Oh, thank you, Jack bought it for me when we went to Key West last weekend on a surprise trip for just the two of us."

 "Jack, what are you doing, man? A trip and a necklace, you're making us all look bad."

The entire table laughs.

Jack holds up his glass to his wife and utters, "Well boys, you know what they say, happy wife, happy life."

Yeah, I could see why so many men and women buy into this myth. If you're a guy, the theory is you will be happy if you give her what she wants. It's simple. If you're a woman, well, who wouldn't want that?

When a man gives his wife everything she wants or does whatever she wants, all for the sole purpose of keeping her happy, is he making himself happy? He may be keeping the peace, and he may desire peace, but isn't he giving up something too? And isn't he then compromising? And what did I say about compromise and marriage? Go back and reread if you need to refresh the idea. Yes, the husband buys himself some peace or time out for "good behavior," or maybe he gets more sex. But this barter scenario will, over time, erode a man's self-worth and authenticity. The only thing he will see himself good for, is doing what his wife wants. It's not fair to him, and it's not fair to his wife either, if you think about it.

Marriage should be about two individuals coming together. Life is a journey. Your spouse is your travel buddy, not your butler. In this modern-day, we are all about equality, and as I said previously, it's never a perfect 50/50 split, but you can get it pretty close with open communication and respect for one another. It's hard to respect someone who gives you what you want so you won't bug him. As a woman, I want an honest, respectful spouse, who loves me and himself. It's hard to respect someone who makes himself a doormat. Temporarily the happy wife, happy life scenario will work for both. Then, it will only work for the wife. This time is usually when many men seek affairs, have a mid-life crisis, or worse, fall into depression and misery. The myth should be, a happy husband and happy wife, happy life.

Takeaway: Just as you don't give a screaming child candy to achieve peace, you shouldn't give your spouse what they want just to preserve happiness. Don't think that this myth is a long-term guarantor of wedded bliss. How could it be? Giving of yourself and not being true to what you want will inevitably erode your love like a cliff in California during mud season.

It's noble and commendable to want your wife to be happy, but only if what you're giving makes you happy too. I do not mean quid pro quo. I mean, if what they are asking is what you want too. For example, if your wife wants to go for a bike ride, and you do too, then go. But if you had plans and if your wife asks you to go for a bike ride, and you say yes to make her happy, that's not ok. Yes, you've kept the peace, which makes you happy for now, but having to deny what you wanted to do will start chipping away at you. Again, talk it out and find a "win-win" solution.

Myth #29: Kids come first

When the airlines tell you, secure your oxygen mask first, then assist others, why do they tell you this? Well, if you're passed out from lack of oxygen, how can you help anyone? Duh. Okay, what makes you think if you put the kids first and the marriage second, that it will work out for you or the kids? Ah, no one.

Yes, some believe that if you don't put kids first, you are selfish. I will tell you the opposite is true. If you love your kids, you will want them to have a stable home and parents who love each other. That can't happen if you don't put your marriage first. I watched Fixer Upper the other day, and Chip Gains said that they put their marriage first because they are their family's foundation. If they don't work, the family doesn't work. It makes sense, right? Yes, absolutely!

Divorce is not something any child should have to experience. Every child de-serves to grow up in a happy, healthy environment, where they can grow and learn about how a good marriage functions—remember, you learned about love from your parents, and your kids will learn from you. Make your mar-riage a priority, and you are laying the foundation for a happy home. What kid wouldn't benefit from that?

Takeaway: Just as Carrie Underwood says in her commercial, when she's working out, to be her best self for her work, husband, and kids, she needs to make time for herself. To be the best parents you can be, you need to make time for your marriage. Make time to keep your connection alive and well. If your marriage is solid and loving, then your kids will flourish from that. They will learn from your example, be strong, and independent and won't fall for the many myths we debunked in this book. Putting your marriage first goes hand in hand with making your kids a priority.

Myth #30: If you fall out of love, get divorced

People fall out of love. It's a fact of life. Many couples, I see, complain that either one or both of them don't feel in love anymore. But the good news is, it doesn't have to be the end. Falling out of love is not a terminal illness. Your marriage can recover and thrive better than before.

I've talked a lot in this chapter about the importance of connection for a couple. Couples with a strong bond and love for one another are that way because they maintain their emotional connection. These feelings for one another then feed into their ability to be free, open, and good communicators. It's what I call the circle of love—the greater the connection, the better the communication, and the better the communication, the greater the connection. When the marriage circle of love is broken, spouses start to live parallel lives, communicate less, and fall out of love easier.

At this point, when the communication and connection break down, spouses will close themselves off further, draw inward, or go the opposite direction and project their hurt outward. Either reaction creates an equal and opposite reaction from the other spouse. How do you prevent your circle of love from becoming one of pain and recrimination?

Find your calm and give yourself what you need to heal. But then sit down and think about the things you loved about this person. What made you fall in love in the first place? Can you find those traits again? Can you accept that sometimes people we love can cause us pain and that eventually, you will have to forgive?

Once you can be honest about how you feel and what you love about them, start working on "liking" them again. Make time to do something together that you both enjoy. Share with your spouse and try to get back the friendship first. The effort will lead back to love. Then try to incorporate touching. Physical contact will help the healing process and allow you to get back to being more intimate with one another, even if sex isn't in the cards right away. The goal, however, should be to get back to a healthy sex life, which will also bring those parallel lines back to a circle of love and caring between you two.

Takeaway: Just as you don't throw the baby out with the bathwater, don't throw your marriage away because you aren't feeling in love with your spouse. The love is there. It doesn't go away as quickly as we think. Sometimes, we must find love again and bring it back to our lives. Take the following steps to fall in love again:

- Make each other a priority.
- Take time to do things you both like together.
- Share your lives even if you are hesitant to open up.
- Show physical affection. Touch is a great healer.
- Be open and honest. Don't hold back or bury your head in the sand.
- If you are on the attack all the time, then stop. Be calm and listen.

Once you can find your love and respect for one another again, the circle of love gets restored, and harmony is achieved. You will also have the tools in your wheelhouse to repair things again, should you find yourself in the same situation. Life is an iterative process of learning and growing. Don't give up on something because it gets complicated. Your marriage deserves the effort to get it back on track.

"Marriage has no guarantees. If that's what you're looking for, go live with a car battery."
- Erma Bombeck, American comedian

So often, weddings override the true meaning of getting married. The excitement of becoming engaged leads directly to planning the "big day." But stepping into roles of husband and wife has little to nothing to do with a ceremony and reception. And many couples put more energy into planning the event than thinking about their future as a couple.

Marriage is about two individuals who come together for a common goal, joining their lives, families, and friends forever. It's about the two of them sustaining their individuality while growing as a couple. It's not about making each other happy, but more so, adding to each other's happiness. And it's not about changing each other, but about each person adapting to a new way of living as one unit.

I tell my patients who are about to marry or have been recently married, they should be kind to themselves and each other as they move through this life event. It's something huge and beautiful. But it's also complex and trying. So, be kind, stay focus on what's important, try to remain connected, and communicate—keep that circle of love alive and well for a long and happy marriage.

CHAPTER 7 –
IGNORE, FIGHT, OR FLIGHT?

Could you imagine being a plumber without a wrench, a carpenter without a hammer, or a doctor without a stethoscope? No, of course not. And could you ride your bike without pedals, ski without skis, or play golf without clubs? No, of course not. Why then get married without any equipment or tools to help you navigate the sometimes-difficult marital waters?

I recently heard a story about a young couple with four children. They were married and divorced from each other twice. This couple is currently trying to get back together for a third go. Their marriage is riddled with emotional abuse and controlling behavior and hasn't shown any signs of improvement. What makes them think that a third time will yield any better results? If they don't have any practical tools in their bag, they still won't fix any issues that arise this time around.

Emotional or physical hurt, deceit, lies, control issues, and indifference are just a few of the things in life that can rock the boat in any marriage. As a therapist, I have seen so many reasons for couples to walk into my office. One woman threw her husband's clothes all over the front lawn when she caught him having an affair, then set the clothing on fire. One husband threw his wife's phone in the barbeque pit because he felt she texted her mother too much. And another husband sold the family cat because he thought the feline received more attention than he did from his wife. None of these actions are appropriate, but they beg the question: When should a person leave, fight, or look the other way in a marriage?

Is there a standard guideline for when you should throw your hands up and surrender to martyrdom and when you should try and work things out? No. How you resolve issues or resolve them between you and your spouse is both individual and situational. Myths out there should be debunked. I will provide more practical advice so that you can make better, more informed decisions about your union.

My wife and I have been married for 21 years, and without a doubt, the hardest times we've faced were those times when we hated each other." — Andy Richter

---

Myth #31: Have a baby it'll fix everything

Allison couldn't describe the overflowing happiness she felt when she and Mark held baby Tara in their arms. Their whole world had changed overnight. Mark suddenly focused on every need Allison or Tara had. With the slightest whimper or movement, Mark jumped up to hold the baby and make sure Allison got her rest. This was the direct opposite of who he was for the first two years of their marriage. Back then, Mark worked long hours, and he filled his off hours with golf and video games, all but ignoring Allison.

"Ally, once you have a baby, Mark's selfishness will go away!" Allison's mom had professed before Allison gave birth.

Then just two months in, Allison's crying, the baby is fussy, the laundry is piling up, they are almost out of diapers, and Mark's parents say they are coming for the week. Allison is at the end of her emotional rope because "helpful Mark" left the building.

"Mark! Can you help me?"

"What the hell? I've been at work all day, and I am running on no sleep. Can't you deal with it? My mom always did!"

Ouch!

My favorite movie of all time is *Eat, Pray, Love*. Born from a popular book by author Elizabeth Gilbert, this movie encompasses a year she took to find herself. Yes, it's a romantic thought and one I've honestly contemplated. But one of my favorite lines from this movie happens when Elizabeth tells her friend she thinks she wants a baby. And her friend responds, "Having a baby is like getting a tattoo on your face. You kind of have to be committed."

When people talk about or imply that having a kid will fix the issues in their marriage, my face twists like an Aunt Annie's pretzel. What? I am not sure who dreamed up this myth, but it had to have been from someone who never had kids, or at least never had to take care of them every day. Kids are an incredible gift. Yet, the decision to have children should never be entertained lightly.

Mark and Allison's marital problems did not magically disappear after having a child. In fact, the pressures on them increased, and their issues magnified after the baby. Let me be blunt. Kids don't make a marriage work better. On the contrary, children make you have to work harder to keep your marriage together. Babies and kids add to life's demands, and even though they bring immense joy, that joy will never fix the cracks in a marriage.

I can hear you thinking: *Is she saying don't have kids, or you'll end up divorcing?* Relax, that isn't even close to what I am saying. Having kids is a significant life decision, right up there with deciding to get married. What I am saying is that the decision process to have or not have children should never include the statement: "Having kids will improve my marriage." No comment could be further from the truth. Instead, have children because you want them and are willing to make them a priority in your life. And have children knowing that there will be additional stress on you as a couple.

Takeaway: I've honestly seen people take longer to decide if they should get a dog than if they should have a baby. When you are trying to determine if you are ready to have kids or not, stop and contemplate all that it means, some will tell you that having children is selfless. I don't see it this way. Having children is a selfish act because it fulfills a desire you have. However, being a good parent is a selfless act because it takes making the kids a priority.

Kids are a beautiful gift, and when you're ready to take on the responsibility, go for it. But do not do it if you think it will save your marriage or change your spouse. Having a baby will add more stress, lack of sleep, financial constraints, and physical demands to your life. Any problems you had before the child will be there afterward and will most likely get worse, not better, without a conscious effort to improve them.

Myth #32: Love hurts

How many times have you gotten off the treadmill or out of a Pilates class dripping with sweat and heard someone say, "No pain, no gain?" But does the same thought of "feeling the burn" hold true for romance? Well, if you've read Shakespeare or Emily Bronte, for example, it does.

Romeo and Juliet or *Wuthering Heights* are all about tortuous love and promote the idea that you will feel extreme lows and extreme highs if you love someone—there is no middle calm ground. Somehow, there is this myth that if your love life doesn't resemble a ride on a rollercoaster, then you aren't experiencing true love.

Even in more modern stories, like in the *Twilight* series, we see this myth promoted between Bella and Edward. When Bella breaks up with Edward, she says, "It's like a huge hole has been punched through my chest. But in a way, I'm glad. The pain is the only reminder that he was real." Fun to read and watch? Yes. But do not think that you must have that intensity level for your relationship to be meaningful. Again, this is only for books and movies. Real love provides a haven, a place for you to be vulnerable, and a place where you feel supported.

Do you find when your spouse leaves you, you fall into depths of depression until they come back? When they return, do you feel like you're on such a high, like you're floating out of the stratosphere? Or when you are together, do you go from huge fights to equally large make-up sessions? If any of these scenarios ring home, do not interpret these reactions as:

- Proving your love for that person.
- Are common for lovers.

I often have patients who believe their tumultuous relationship is that way because it's supposed to be like that. No, it isn't. I've known individuals to flee a relationship because it was too easy or comfortable for them. Let me tell you a fact, for long-term relationships to work well, they must contain a level of comfort and be emotionally stable. That is not to say that these relationships don't have times of anger, sadness, or hurt. They do. The difference is they don't have them *all the time*.

If your partner harms you physically or emotionally in the name of love, it's a lie. Again, love shouldn't hurt you repeatedly. Love shouldn't feel like someone flicking an on-off switch constantly. If you think this way about your relationship, get help from a close, but objective friend, family, or even better, from a licensed therapist.

Takeaway: A healthy relationship feels like driving on a long stretch of road, where occasionally, you may have a turn or hit a bump. But, if your relationship feels like you're driving up and down Lombard Street in San Francisco constantly, then it's NOT a sign of love. It's a sign of distress.

Although entertaining, Stephanie Meyer's *Twilight* series does nothing but promote this myth of "love hurts." Bella and Edward are written as tumultuous lovers who are so in love that they will engage in risky, suicidal, or depressive behaviors. As a therapist who works with teens—huge readers of this material—I find her writing careless and without understanding her readership. She promotes this idea of a love so intense you would die to gain peace. Not at all what our teens should hear.

Love isn't easy, as I've stated before, but love shouldn't constantly hurt either. Love takes work, but it shouldn't be so exhausting that it leaves you depleted for little else in your life. If you find yourself either physically or emotionally abused, do not let anyone tell you that:

- Your feelings are invalid.
- They hurt you because they love you.

Both above statements are false under every circumstance. If you are in a relationship like this, seek help from a licensed therapist as soon as possible or talk to someone you love. Either way, get help. Love shouldn't be a steady stream of pain.

Myth #33: If your partner is flirtatious, it's ok, as long as they come home to you

I happened to be out with some friends at a bar one night, just relaxing and catching up on what everyone had been doing. Across the way from my group, sitting at the bar, was a good-looking couple. I noticed how the guy would lean back and watch a pretty girl would walk by. He did this about four or five times, and his girlfriend seemed to ignore the behavior.

"Rachel, are you with us?"

"Yeah. You see that guy over there at the bar. His girlfriend keeps talking to him, but he's more interested in other girls, and he won't stop talking to the bartender."

"So, you're not paying attention?"

"I am. I just find this interesting. I can't figure out if the girlfriend is ok with it or doesn't notice."

"She's probably used to it and just ignores it. Not worth the argument."

Just as my friend made that statement, the girlfriend at the bar stands up, throws her drink in the guy's face, and walks out.

"Hmmm, well, guess she noticed," my friend said.

"Yep, she reached her limit!" Our waitress chimed in, delivering our second round.

When is it okay to flirt? When is flirting "crossing of the relationship line?" I get this question a lot. My answer: It depends on the couple and their tolerances. Some might not care if you openly flirt as long as you don't touch. Others may be ok with you doing some playful non-intimate touching even. While some may say no way to any flirting of any kind, even a glance in another's direction is a no-no.

Modern technology has added another wrinkle to this flirting controversy for couples. When is it okay to text with someone other than your partner? I am referring to anyone who could potentially be of romantic interest. For example, let's say your husband's best friend texts you and wants to meet up for a drink. If you text back and accept, is that crossing a line? What if your husband's friend text's you a funny joke, and you respond with a witty, flirty comeback? Is that crossing the line?

Even though these lines or tolerance thresholds are different for each individual, some red flags may indicate you should check your actions, such as the following: When you do anything in secret, it's probably crossing a line. If you are doing everything you can to make sure your partner doesn't find out you've been texting another person. If your words or correspondence have a sexual agenda, or your communication fulfills a fantasy or creates a fantasy life for you. Below are additional situations that could also indicate your actions have crossed a line:

- If your communication contains sexual undertones.
- If you're spending a lot of time conversing with this other person. Far more time than you give your spouse.
- If this relationship is meeting your needs, such as you are sharing personal thoughts or ideas with this other person, but not your husband or wife, then that's a problem.
- If you're rationalizing the other person is "just a friend." You don't justify innocent behavior.
- If your partner voices a concern about the time you spend talking or texting with this individual, then it's crossing a line.
- If your friends tell you, they think you are spending too much time with this individual.
- If your intentions are wrong, for example, let's say you are trying to escape your marriage because you feel unappreciated. So, you seek validation from this other person.

Takeaway: When you walk out of a store, do you stop and ask yourself, "Did I steal anything?" No, you don't. You know if you stole something, or you didn't. Whenever you find yourself questioning if your actions cross the line, then there is a good chance you are. If that still doesn't make it clear, then ask yourself one of the following questions:

- If I were my spouse, how would I feel about my texting or conversing with someone in the way that I am?
- If I were my spouse, how would I feel about texting or conversing with someone as frequently as I do?
- Does the time I spend talking, emailing, or texting with this other person take away from my time with my spouse?
- Does the time I spend talking, emailing, or texting provide me with something I should be getting from my spouse?
- If I were my spouse, would I ask me to stop this behavior?
- If I were my friend, would I see my behavior as questionable?

Whenever you can practice empathy and see yourself through someone else's lens, you get a better, more accurate view of your actions.

Myth #34: Forgive and forget

The phone wouldn't stop ringing, and Claire finally picked it up, frustrated as she was trying to finish an article for her paper's deadline. "Hello?"

Silence.

Her finger on the off button, but before she pushed it, "Claire?"

"Yes, this is Claire."

Silence.

"Can I help you?"

"My name is Ellen Katts."

"Ok. I'm sorry I don't recognize the name."

"I work with your husband, Tom."

By the time Tom walked through the door later that night, there wasn't a light on anywhere. No food delivery bags were piled on the kitchen counter, which was their norm on the days that Claire had tight deadlines.

"Hello!" Tom yelled, placing his backpack on the hallway bench like always.

He rounded the corner and stuck to the refrigerator door was a note he never expected to get.

> *Tom,*
>
> *I got a call today from Ellen. You've hurt me beyond words, and I expect you to be packed and gone before I get home in two days. I will be divorcing you immediately. I will never be one of those wives who forgives and forgets!*
>
> *Claire*

In marriage, when one person hurts the other badly, there is the assumption that everything will be fine once the other spouse forgives them and forgets. This is not true. Forgiving and forgetting aren't a package deal. They are mutually exclusive actions. So, for the couples that come into my office, where forgiveness may be necessary, we must redefine the term. And I tell them to throw "forgetting" in the trash—it doesn't belong here.

For emphasis, I like to start by stating what forgiveness is *not*: Forgiveness is not accepting or allowing your partner's behavior. Forgiveness is not minimizing their behavior or making excuses for it. Forgiveness is not reconciliation. Forgiveness is most definitely not a feeling. And again, forgiveness is not forgetting.

Forgiveness *is* a process. Forgiveness is a conscious choice to move forward while acknowledging the hurt and pain. Consequences are also crucial to the forgiving process. The person who committed the act must pay the consequences. Depending on what they do, the repercussions will range from legal to monetary to relational. Recognition and outcomes are critical for the healing process to occur. This path may take time, so remember to be kind to yourself.

Again, this point begs repeating: Forgetting has no place in the process of forgiveness. The process works best when you don't forget. When you can address and discuss what was done to hurt you, you will move the healing process along much easier.

Note that you can forgive someone and not reconcile with them. Reconciliation depends upon the following elements:

- There is a desire of the individuals involved.
- The hurt inflicted.
- The desire of the offender to face their consequences and move forward.
- The presence of forgiveness.

Takeaway: For an individual who has been harmed by the one they love, to move forward and provide forgiveness consciously, they must understand what forgiveness is not:

- Forgiveness is not forgetting.
- Forgiveness is not condoning.
- Forgiveness is not minimizing.
- Forgiveness is not a feeling.
- Forgiveness is not reconciliation.

Stanford University psychologist, Fred Luskin, has defined forgiveness as "…a conscious, deliberate decision to release feelings of resentment or vengeance toward a person or group who has harmed you, regardless of whether they deserve your forgiveness" (Ferreira, 2019). Forgiveness is the process of releasing your hurt. It's like the process of applying a tourniquet to a bleeding artery or vein. Forgiveness is more about *your* healing than the other person's. If you can release your pain, throw it out, and take back your happiness, you will heal. Anger and recrimination won't do that for you.

Myth #35: Never go to bed angry

A lack of sleep is one of the leading causes of conflict. Have you ever noticed when you are exhausted that the littlest things bother you? For example, the way your spouse brushes their teeth or chews gum can make you want to claw their eyes out. Or, when your spouse tells you they just put spent a lot of money on something you see as "extra," and it makes you fly off the handle. This is because being tired diminishes your ability to filter information calmly and accurately.

So, here are my thoughts: If you are tired, I never recommend discussing anything serious with your partner—there's a good chance it won't end well, no matter how much you want to get something off your chest. This myth is one of the worst pieces of advice! It encourages you and your spouse to stay up and either hash things out or until one person gives in just to get sleep.

Curious about the impact of sleep on conflict, I did a study with some of my willing patients. I brought them in and asked each of them how they slept the night before. Then I sent each couple off to resolve a current issue in their relationship. In the cases where at least one person had a poor night's sleep, the couples were less understanding of each other and demonstrated a much harder time resolving their issue. Conversely, I've read about others who have done studies on sleep and conflict where they found that going to bed without resolving the issue led to poor sleep.

Sleep is not the only factor that impacts conflict. Stress, lack of time, hunger, physical fatigue, or illness can leave our fuse short. Yes, being hangry is a real thing. If your husband leaves a trail of clothing from the bedroom to the bathroom or uses the last of the toilet paper, leaving you stranded on the toilet may send you over the edge if you're not your sweet self. Often, those minor annoyances during the day become significant issues when you are in some way physically or emotionally depleted.

The Gottman Institute's Love Lab did a study where they interrupted couples, mid-argument, and asked them to read a magazine for 30 minutes. When instructed to go back to the argument, they had calmed down—their dispositions in a better place. The couples communicated much more effectively and resolved their issues easier. They were proving that perhaps, taking a break and going to bed might bring you to a better place in the morning.

Take a breather. For those who think that leaving an issue overnight will be detrimental to your union, I call foul. It all goes back to connection. As we discussed in the previous chapter, if you are connected, your communication is strong, and therefore so is your love. Keep that connection up and when you have issues that need discussing, do it when you are both in a good place mentally and physically. You will have a better conversation, a more respectful exchange, and a more positive outcome.

Takeaway: Just as you would send an out-of-control child for a time out to cool down, adults need to do the same thing. As the saying goes, "It will all look better in the morning," allowing your conflict to take a break is a good thing. When you can address things when your mental and physical states are in good condition, the outcome will be more favorable for all involved.

You put off tasks, like paying bills, or calling your mother because your mind is too cluttered, or you're starving, or you don't have enough time, and so on. Do the same with conflicts. Take a breather. Get your body and mind in a good place before you work on resolving an issue. Often, you might just find that what you thought was huge while you were hangry was nothing to argue about. Let's put off World War III in your house by instituting a calm down period, then revisit when you are ready.

Myth #36: Admitting you're wrong is a sign of weakness

Who likes to admit they did something wrong? No one. It's as if you're transported back to your youth, you hunch over, you squirm, and you hem and haw while you wait for the repercussions of your actions. Even the so-called strong, tough exterior types struggle with the awkwardness of coming clean—let's face it, it's not easy to do.

This offsetting feeling of not wanting to face your wrongdoings takes incredible inner strength for any individual. It's much easier to run, hide, or conceal your misdoings than to admit to them. That's why I have never understood this completely erroneous myth.

When I was much younger, I remember a disagreement between my parents. My dad's voice escalated as he grew more and more determined to present his point. As a teen, I stayed in my room, listening to them shout their opinions. Although my dad had analytical insights, he projected a feeling of dismissiveness to my mom's points. After a short while, they stopped talking and went to different parts of the house.

Five minutes later, to my father's credit, I heard him seek out my mom and apologize for his behavior. Even though his points were valid, he understood his delivery was wrong and hurtful. He'd made a mistake. We don't think of our parents making mistakes, and for me, his actions during the argument shocked me. But then, how he handled his error afterward only increased my respect for him. It took an act of strength for him to give an apology and accept responsibility for his actions.

How do you handle being wrong? Next time you do something wrong, think about these benefits of admitting your mistakes:

- It's a sign of strength. Although admitting you're wrong can make you feel weak or vulnerable, it takes power to feel this way and try not to repeat your actions.
- Coming forward before you "get caught" shows you value the other individual and that you're sincere about your apology.
- Realizing you did something wrong allows you to see your actions more clearly and use this time as an opportunity to grow.
- It can improve your communication with your partner and others. This simple act of apologizing will give insight into how to best communicate under stress. Being vulnerable and forthcoming will inspire your love to do the same with you. It sets a precedent.

Let's say you've hidden the credit card bill from your spouse and paid it before they could see purchases you know they would have questioned. When they ask if you got the bill, you start to squirm and feel guilty—your spouse notices and waits for you to stop hemming and hawing and come clean. You finally muster the strength and tell them and offer an apology for your behavior.

What have you done? You've admitted you were wrong and apologized. But as the above benefits state, you can do more than just blurt out and wait for recrimination. You can take this time to talk with your spouse about why you did it and what the two of you can do going forward to mitigate this from reoccurring. For example, maybe you discover that you hid the bill because you feel your spouse controls what you buy too much. You've both gotten to the root of the issue. Now, you can discuss how to change the situation.

When I have patients tell me they refuse to take the blame for something—even though they did it—because it will make them weak, I tell them: You aren't admitting defeat and surrendering to the enemy here. There is a term the military uses called a calculated retreat. This term is when you step back and regroup. It gives you and your partner time to take a breather. You aren't defeated, but you are accepting responsibility for your actions and refocusing on the future.

As in the case of my parents, my dad didn't accept defeat. He apologized for what he did wrong but still stood by what his points were in the argument. He showed true strength and character, which allowed my mom to see his sincerity and feel comfortable moving forward in discussion with him. They came to a resolution and developed more profound respect along the way—a win-win.

But what would have happened if my dad had not apologized. Well, resentment on my mom's part would have grown, future disagreements would suffer because she would still hold the feeling that he wasn't hearing her. And the communication between them would have suffered. As we talked about in the previous chapters, communication is part of that love cycle. If you don't feel you're heard or valued, your communication suffers, and then your connection suffers.

Takeaway: As with anything, the more you do it, the better you get at it. This is not me saying go out and screw up repeatedly and just apologize. That is certainly not okay. Everyone should try to be their best self all day, every day. However, we are all human. Everyone makes mistakes, but what separates the strong from the weak is how we handle ourselves afterward.

In debunking this myth, we have talked about the value of apologizing, but here are the steps to follow:

1. Don't be defensive. Do not start justifying why you did something.

2. Take complete ownership. Refrain from blame. Don't turn it around and make it come across as though your partner is the reason you

screwed up—no gaslighting.

3.   Choose the right time to talk with your partner. As we discussed previously, knowing when to best approach your spouse is a critical tool for a positive exchange.

4.   Let your partner express their feelings about what you did. Go back to steps one and two and don't get defensive but take ownership.

If you follow these steps in your discussion, although you did something wrong, you and your relationship will come out a winner—lose the battle, win the war!

Myth #37: Staying together for the kids is best

"I can't listen to another story about how bad Todd is!" Audrey said to her friends, Ceal and Kirsten.

"Yeah, Janet, talks about him non-stop. At first, I thought it was Todd being a jerk, but three years of listening to how bad he is and her not doing anything about it, has me wondering if it is him. He always seems so beaten down," Ceal lamented.

Kirsten added, "Well, she says they're staying together for the twins, but they don't sleep together, they take separate vacations, and they argue constantly. Not sure how that works for the kids?"

"It doesn't!" Ceal and Audrey say in unison.

This is not a fictional story, but a story of a real couple living separately within their home, claiming they are doing so for their kids. I can't help but think of how living in this environment has impacted these kids. I am not saying that the couple doesn't love their children. I am saying that the lack of love and respect for each other does filter down.

I recently talked with someone who recounted how during her childhood, her parents fought endlessly. She talked about how she "waited for the shoe to drop" every time her parents were together. This woman recounted that one day she asked her mom why she and her dad fought so much. The mom answered, "Well, I think it's healthy for you to see us argue. It's real."

Both these scenarios present a volatile existence. If your kids hear you constantly bicker, sense your distance, and your dislike for one another, what does that teach them? Well, it causes insecurity in the home, it changes how these kids see a loving marriage, and they, most likely, will either grow up to repeat what they've seen or go to the other extreme to avoid it.

As for the twins in the first story, we won't know how that will affect them. But the woman in the second story is grown, married, and divorced. This woman tells of how she married a narcissist just like her father. When her husband would explode, she remembered her mother's words and did everything not to repeat that environment for her children. She used the peace at any price approach and lost herself and her voice in the process, until one day she couldn't take it anymore and kicked her abuser to the curb.

Why am I telling these sad tales? Because although I believe in marriage, I also know that there are times when it's unhealthy for you to stay in the union, even with kids involved. Yes, parents who stay together are best, **if and only if** they foster a loving environment in the home and demonstrate respect and love for their union. If they can't do that, then it's time to ask: Is this benefitting the children?

Part of making your kids a priority means you need to put yourself in their position and see the world through their eyes—employ empathy. A survey done by a family law organization found that 82% of people from age 14 to 22, who were products of divorce, stated that they preferred their parents to be apart and happy, versus together and miserable (Bowcott, 2015).

If you think you are masking your contempt, misery, or lack of love for your spouse, think again. Kids may not see you argue, but they are much more intuitive than we give them credit for. Your dismissiveness, snippiness, or overall indifference toward your partner will be picked up. And guess what, when your children grow up, they will repeat what they see or make a conscious choice to go in the opposite direction to the point of potentially putting themselves in a difficult situation.

Kids who grow up in a home filled with love and respect, whether both parents are together or not, are far better prepared for life than kids who have two parents in a home that is filled with resentment and unhappiness. They see it, sense it, and absorb it—you aren't doing anything for them.

Now, this is not me pushing you to get a divorce. The first step to any discord or movement in that direction should cause you to stop and take some stock of your life. This is a good time for you to seek counseling and see if you can restore the love for each other, you once had. It will take some work, but in many cases, it can be done. If nothing else, you will set an example for your children and show them that you love yourself, them, and your partnership enough to try and make it work. If it still doesn't work after that, and you divorce, then put the kids' needs first. Put aside your contempt for each other and be the best co-parents you can be. In the end, it's not about living together. It's about loving the children enough to give them a happy life filled with your love and support.

Takeaway: The question shouldn't be, "Should we stay together for the kids?" The question should be, "Is this the life I want for my children?" Your kids deserve you to make a conscious choice to work on your marriage or to dissolve it by analyzing the life you are giving them. Are you raising them in a loving environment that values and supports each of you? And if you stay together, are you willing to put in the work to make the environment better? Think about your answers. Be open and honest with your kids and let them express their feelings openly and without recrimination. Family looks different for everyone, but love and respect should always be the foundation.

Myth #38: Staying in a relationship is better than being alone

If you have ever watched a Dr. Phil show or read any of his books on relationships, there is one question he asks his guests or his patients who are unhappy with their relationship: "How's that working for you?"

I find myself saying those exact words when patients come in and complain about their spouse or life partner and yet have no desire to change anything. For example, it's not uncommon for a couple to sit in therapy and say:

Patient one: "All he does is drink and go to bed at night."

Patient two: "All she does is spend money and whine about how I don't listen."

Me: "Do you, "patient one," tell "patient two" how you feel?" and "Do you, "patient two," tell "patient one" how you feel?"

Patient one: "Why should I? It's not like anything will change!"

Patient two: "I don't want to change."

Me: "Do you want this marriage to be better?"

Patient one and two exchange looks. I have just asked them a question they can't answer. They have been together so long they've grown comfortable in their misery. Or, in the paraphrased words of Dr. Phil, it's somehow working for them.

Patient two: "Isn't this just marriage? I mean, who wants to be alone?"

Ding-ding! It works because they don't want to be single.

Me: "Does alone always mean you're sitting in a room by yourself? Alone can also mean being with someone and lacking a real connection? So, in a way, if you're not connected, then aren't you alone already?"

Silence.

Another question they can't answer. Eventually, I will attempt to get the couple to see that you either work to make it better or leave. But the truth is that many remain in an unhappy union because the fear of being alone is far worse than their current reality. Plus, there is an innate comfort in their unhappiness.

What's that saying, "Better the devil you know than the devil you don't?" I hear it all the time from couples who tell me they would rather have their issues than be back out in the dating world. Instead, what they should be saying, "I'd rather be with my partner and working on improving our life than being out in the dating world."

Takeaway: Only you and your partner can answer the question of staying or leaving. But either way, this myth is more about a person's fears or sheer laziness. The truth is, if you and your partner aren't connecting, then you are already alone. Wouldn't you rather be on your own and living in a happier environment than sitting next to someone every night and cringing every time they speak?

I once had someone tell me she knew her friend was headed for divorce when she looked at her and said, "The way he chews his food makes me want to stab him with my fork!" Her friend eventually did divorce, but it took her many years to come to that decision.

It's not something to take lightly, and as a marriage therapist, I am not trying to sell one way or the other. Every couple's situation is different. The decision to stay together or to leave varies, but it should never be made from a place of fear or laziness. You shouldn't remain in a relationship to avoid being alone or because you don't want to go through the process of divorce. Your decision to stay should be because you value your relationship and desire to get back to a deep connection with your partner. You should be willing and ready to do the work to rekindle your fire and move forward toward happiness.

If you find yourself in this situation and are trying to decide whether to work on your relationship or leave it, make sure you have your support network. Nurture those external, non-romantic friendships and family ties. Having outside support is critical to help you through tricky times and provide you with the feeling of not being alone.

Ultimately, it would help if you accepted that you will have times of loneliness, despite having a perfect network of friends and family. It's just part of life. Know that even happily married individuals experience loneliness from time to time. Accept it, embrace it, and keep moving forward.

Myth #39: They can change

When someone attends an AA meeting, and they introduce themselves, they stand up and state their name, followed by, "I am an alcoholic." Why do they have to do this? Because you can't change what you don't acknowledge. You have a better chance to teach a blind man to drive than you do to change your partner. You can't and won't ever be able to change another person.

I hear others say that they'll change after this happens, or once work stops being stressful, or after they are financially secure, they will be happy. Stop kidding yourself! Unless your partner is willing to look inward, analyze their actions, and admit they need to change, change will never occur.

Here's a story: Melinda and Kyle walked into the restaurant and were seated at their favorite table. Melinda picked up the menu to see the specials.

The waiter came by, and Kyle said, "We are going to have the scallops and start with a bottle of Pinot, please."

Melinda put her menu down. She was furious because Kyle chose for her all the time, and she had been talking to him about it for months, and it hadn't gotten any better. "What have I been telling you?"

"What?" Kyle said, looking through his phone.

"Stop making decisions for me."

"Do you like scallops?"

"Yes."

"Then what's the problem. When Charlie puts scallops as the special, it means he got them fresh that day. They aren't a normal item on the menu."

"That's not my point!"

"So, order something else and stop complaining!"

"No, I want the scallops!"

Kyle shook his head and went back to his phone.

"We need to talk about the blinds for the beach house."

"I had the contractor order them already." Kyle snipped.

"What? I can't take you skirting around me all the time and making decisions for the both of us!"

"Huh? I got the ones you wanted. Relax!"

Kyle wasn't getting what Melinda was telling him. He couldn't see his ways as controlling or dismissive. Melinda became more and more furious over his lack of understanding. Will she ever change him? Nope. Kyle has to want to change, but it will first take him recognizing in himself what Melinda sees.

What do you do if you are Melinda? Well, first, stop trying to melt an iceberg with a blow dryer. It won't work. Next, you will need to look inward. I am not suggesting that you blame yourself for another's actions, but you must under-stand and accept how those actions affect you. This is called self-investigation, and it has nothing to do with blame.

When you turn the question into yourself, ask: "What does this person's behav-ior or actions trigger in me? Identifying what the other person's behaviors do to you, how it gives you pain. Identifying your hurt will show compassion for it. It's not condoning the other person's actions or being permissive. It's giving yourself the power to control what happens inside you. It's a time to free yourself from unwanted responses to your partner's behavior.

In Melinda's case, by recognizing what her husband's behavior does to her, she will be able to identify her pain and the cause. That action alone will free her from this cycle. This is not to say she is okay with Kyle's actions. She is taking back her power to name her pain and identify its cause. From there, she can control her responses. Self-awareness is the best tool to combat your suffering and allow Melinda to express herself more effectively to Kyle.

Takeaway: If you could only change someone else the way you change your underwear, well, wouldn't life be fabulous? It may seem simple, but the best anecdote for another's poor behavior or actions is not hoping they will change. It is actually for you to self-reflect. Looking inside yourself and identifying the source of your troubles and altering your response to them is an act of self-love. Taking control of yourself takes others out of control.

Myth #40: Time heals all wounds

When you're wheeled into the emergency room for a gunshot wound, does the doctor declare, "Ah, just give it time? Time heals everything!" Ah, no. Well, time does not heal everything. Time may lessen the pain in some instances, but it will never eradicate it.

Think back to when you were younger, and your sibling said or did something mean to you. Those words or actions hurt, and you still wince at them today. Some may even taunt you and affect your self-esteem.

So, when you have significant life changes, such as divorce or your spouse cheating on you: Do you just tell yourself to wait it out? No, of course not. You should first be kind to yourself and give yourself time to come to terms with your truth. Then, if forgiveness (see our myth on forgiving and forgetting) is required, grant it only when you are ready to heal. And lastly, seek out the help of a therapist who can help you get your life back on track.

Takeaway: Just as ignoring the pain of a broken arm won't make it heal, waiting out the pain of a broken heart needs more than time. To properly heal, you must be ready to walk through the process of forgiveness and accepting of the life change.

Myth #41: You'll always stay in love in a relationship

He looked at her knowing she was the one. She didn't just walk, she floated, she didn't just smile, she shined like the sun, and her words were soft and breathy, like a feather floating on a breeze. Fast forward 15 years, and his beloved walked into the room like an elephant running from a mouse. Her voice screeched her latest complaint, making him wish he'd purchased earplugs. *The honeymoon is officially over*, he thought.

Later that week, he came home to a quiet house. His wife was reading in the living room, and he walked in and asked how her day was. She softly answered him and suggested they go out for dinner and have some alone time. Before finishing dinner, they held hands and reconnected over a shared piece of chocolate cake—and just like that, he was in love all over again.

If you think that the feeling you have when love is new will last for 30 or 40 years, you are setting yourself up for failure. The proverbial honeymoon period won't last forever. Love is truly an emotion that comes and goes as it pleases, sometimes without your ability to explain it. You are not always going to see your partner as perfect. The way they pile crap on the counter or constant farting will have you envisioning their demise, but in a flash, they will take out the garbage or be sweet to your nagging mother, and you immediately feel that warm, tingly feeling again.

Many complain they have lost the thrill in their long-term relationships, but excitement gets replaced with security and companionship. Plus, there is excitement around falling in love all over again, never knowing when or how it will happen. Yes, the emotion of love is puzzling, but although it changes for us over the years, there is a comfort of knowing it will continue to show up again and again.

Takeaway: Just because you plot your husband's death as he keeps you awake with his snoring, it doesn't mean you won't fall in love with him again when he surprises you with a weekend away. Life is inconsistent, and so is love. Our emotions can change on a dime, and we may not know why. But when the connection is deep between you and your partner, you can count on those feelings returning at some point. And if they don't produce on their own, then, as we said earlier in the book, find a way to reconnect and create the moment for yourself, your spouse, and your marriage.

Myth #42: If they can't handle your worst, they don't deserve your best

"I make mistakes, I am out of control, and at times hard to handle, but if you can't handle me at my worst, then you sure as hell don't deserve me at my best." This quote by Marilyn Monroe was shortened to, "If they can't handle your worst, they don't deserve your best," and it's on wall art and t-shirts all over. Yes, it's cute and funny, but it has no merit, and it's misleading.

Just as I said at the beginning of this book that you shouldn't expect perfection from your mate, it's also wrong to expect them to put up with your baggage. If you're a hot mess and hope them to just take what you're giving, that is unfair. In any relationship, you should always treat the other person with respect and expect the same return. Will there be times you don't? Yes, but you should follow those up with an apology and a promise to do better.

The expectation that your partner should somehow just "deal with your crazy" isn't ok. If you find your feeling this way, think about the damage you're doing to your relationship. If your spouse is the sponge to your messy spillage, then what they are doing is soaking up your issues and creating resentment at the same time. When they can no longer contain their feelings of hurt and frustration, they will seep out, and the repercussions could be devastating.

Takeaway: Just as you wouldn't expect a good parent to take their child's bratty behavior, do not expect your spouse to accept your adult meltdowns. Own your behavior, spend some time to find out why you react or act the way you do at times, and figure out how to be a better you. Then apologize for your actions and do better, just as a parent would expect after a child misbehaves. Thinking that your spouse needs to put up with your hot mess is an unfair expectation and one that could rear its ugly head down the road.

"I love being married. It's so great to find that one special
person you want to annoy for the rest of your life."
- Rita Rudner

Marriage offers that partner with whom to share life's ups and downs. And like life, your union will go through its joys and disappointments. From our debunking of these multiple marriage myths, take away the following advice:

- Keep your expectations realistic.
- Anticipate some dips in the road but flat surfaces too.
- Keep the connection between you strong.
- Keep the conversations open and honest.
- Actively listen to each other.
- Learn to apologize for the actions you did wrong and work to do better.
- Learn that the process of forgiving isn't the same as condoning, but it's essential for your healing.
- Together in misery isn't ok for you or the children.
- Be the best you, you can be. You can only control yourself.
- Your spouse should also follow the previous rules. If they don't, it's time to reevaluate and seek help from a therapist.

Marriage, although work is involved, should be seen as the gift it is. Once you have someone to take this ride through life with, then being each other's emotional supporter and champion should always be the goal. If that describes your marriage, then you are #Blessed.

CHAPTER 8 –
Finances

Andy put down his fork, "Wow, that was delicious!"

Caroline smiled and added, "Yes, it was really good. Do you come here a lot?"

"Only on first dates!" Andy said with a wink and a smirk.

Caroline gave a forced laugh as she casually checked the time on her watch.

The waiter came by, "How was dessert?"

"Amazing," Caroline answered as the waiter picked up the dessert plates and then removed the bill folder from his apron and placed it in the middle of the table.

When the waiter left, Caroline looked at the bill folder and then at Andy. Andy wiped his hands on the cloth napkin and laid it on top of the table. He made no move to pick up the check.

"Well, this was great. Thank you for inviting me here," Caroline said, throwing a subtle hint at Andy's deaf ears.

Andy, looking at his phone, gave the nod.

The waiter returned a few minutes later, reaching for the folder, "I'll be right back with the receipt."

Caroline looked at a distracted Andy and then stopped the waiter, "We haven't—"

"Oh, sorry. I'll come back," the waiter said, putting the bill back down but closer to Andy this time.

Andy stood up, "I'll be right back."

Caroline took her credit card out, slipped it into the folder, and called the waiter back over.

The waiter smiled and shook his head at Andy's seat. Caroline said a quick goodnight before heading back to her apartment.

"You paid?" Caroline's roommate asked.

"Yep!" Caroline shouted as she hung up her coat and kicked off her shoes.

"He didn't say anything when you paid the bill? What a schmuck!"

"Nope," Caroline said, flopping on the couch. "But it's ok."

"Why?" her roommate asked, adjusting her position in her beanbag chair.

"I sent him a request for payment on Venmo."

Do you agree with how Caroline handled the situation? Do you think Andy should have paid, and if so, is it because he invited Caroline or because he was a man? How you answer these questions will give you insight into your preconceived notions about romance and finances. Yes, we can all agree dollars and dates create awkward moments. But just as a conservative will eventually cross paths with a liberal, so too will money meet romance. You can't avoid it, but you can prepare for it.

I purposely waited to talk about finances until the end of the book because it covers every aspect of your romantic life, from dating to marriage. Whether you're on a first date, living together, or married, money will be a topic you will have to deal with. So, let's dive right into the murky waters of the, who, what, when, where, and how of paying for life's expenses.

"Are you free tomorrow? No, I'm Still expensive."
— Anonymous

Myth #43: The guy should pay

In the past, men were expected to take on the role of financial provider even when couples started dating. In modern society, where there is far more equality among genders, the man's part in money is blurry. A man would ask a woman to dinner in decades past, and the expectation was that he would pay. Now, when the bill comes, it can present as an awkward moment. The situation can run from the woman expecting the man to pay to the woman offended if a man offers to pick up the tab. Even though I'm not a man, I feel for them on this issue—it's the wild west out there.

However, The Door Research (2010) found that for heterosexual relationships, where some traditional stereotypes still existed, it's still expected that if a man asks a woman out first, he will pay for their date. The study also found that many modern singles believe it's ok for either party to initiate or pay for the first date, although men still predominately take on the role of the payer (Lever, 2015).

So, what should you do? What is the right way to address who pays on a date? First, be honest from the get-go. If you ask someone out and have personal values that dictate you should pay, let that be known. If you are a guy who wants a life partner who will share all the bills and not conform to old norms, then be upfront from the beginning. If you are a woman who doesn't want a man to pay for her, then let it be known.

But what happens when you are like Caroline, in the example above? What happens if the check is levitating between the two of you and no one is reaching for it; you believe he should pay because he asked you out, but he's not grabbing for the bill? At that point, his lack of action means he doesn't share your view. Take the cue. Offer to pay your half at least. In the end, if he makes you pay, then you have a glimpse into his perspective on finances. If that works for you or it doesn't bother you, then great. If it doesn't work for you, then you move on. This is one of those times you need to be alert to signs. Money is a huge thing to have different views on—it has caused many, many divorces.

When it comes to money and your first few dates, don't try and be someone you're not. Yes, we want to portray the best version of ourselves in the beginning, but I never recommend altering the truth. Don't act like your loaded with cash, if you can barely afford a tin of Altoids—it will never end in your favor. Be your best self, but be who you are, not who you think the other person wants.

If someone just wants you for your money, is that ok with you? I would hope your answer is a resounding, "No, of course not."

If you are upfront about your financial status from the beginning and what your goals are down the road, the other person will respect you. If you come in like a white night paying for everything and then when your ATM eats your card one day, what will happen? Most likely, the other person will feel hurt, not because you can't pay, but because you portrayed yourself as someone different than who you are—never a good way to start a relationship.

Now, in the case where you've been together for a long time, you should have already discussed who pays for what. At this point, you should know what the other person does for a living and their financial situation. But even if you are both bringing in excellent salaries, you should at least share or offer to share the dating expenses. If one person always assumes the other person will pay, then that is selfish and unfair.

When talking about finances, do it with respect and politeness. Talking about money may offend some individuals, so be sure you delicately approach the subject. I suggest taking the following steps when discussing money with your partner:

1. Explain your point. Maybe you want to pay half when you go out, and your boyfriend won't accept it. Calmly explain your side and how that makes you feel.

2. Create understanding. If you feel your dating expenses have been a significant burden on your wallet, let the other person know. You should never go into debt to make someone else happy or because you "feel" like you need to do something.

3. Share a plan. Talk about how, as you move forward in the relationship, you see the expenses being shared or how best to keep the costs down.

4. Never force your opinion on the other person. If you come from two different standpoints, do not force your thoughts down their throat. This may be a juncture where you decide if you're ok with disagreeing or if the chasm between the both of you is too wide.

Takeaway: Broaching the topic of money is about as appealing as taking a bath in ice cubes. But if you ever plan to go on a date, then money inevitably becomes part of the equation. My recommendation for the first few dates is this: If you're being asked out, then go on a date but bring money and be prepared to at least offer to pay half. If this is not your first date, also have cash with you so you can offer to pay. It all comes down to being honest and to having respect for the other person. Don't assume or believe anyone owes you anything.

Myth #44: Keep your finances separate

Chip sat on his friend's couch, hands in his head, "I lost my job two weeks ago. Today I pull in the driveway and see that Jackie had put our living room furniture out for trash pick-up." Chip lifted his head and threw his hands in the air, "Like she just decided we need new furniture! Now? While I'm out of work?"

Chip's friend sat dumbfounded with his wife by his side. Neither knew how to respond. They did a lot of head-nodding while Chip kept talking.

"It's like we are on two different wavelengths when it comes to money. I bet you guys don't have these issues."

"Well, we handle money differently, that's for sure. But when we got married, a lawyer friend told us that most marriages end over money problems. So, we agreed to a plan early on, and we stick to it."

Chip and his wife divorced a few years later. Again, finances played a considerable role in the split. I didn't know Chip or his wife, but I heard this story from their friend, and it's not as uncommon as you may think. According to the *Journal of Divorce and Remarriage*, 40% of couples claim how their spouse handled money was the cause of their divorce. For anyone living together, getting married, or newly married, take this matter seriously. It's time to sit down and have that heart-to-heart with your partner using the steps I lined out in the previous myth (Gjelten, n.d.).

Whether you're living together, engaged, or married, you have three options for handling finances: You can have separate accounts, joint accounts on everything, or use a hybrid of the prior two. As with anything, there are pros and cons to each approach.

For those individuals in a serious relationship and living together, I would only recommend that you split the expenses and keep your finances separate. With the statistics being high for breakups among this group, it's much easier to uncouple when your finances aren't intertwined. Plus, keeping things split down the middle gives each equal footing in the relationship.

Sheri walked over to Craig as he watched the Sunday football game and handed him her phone, "Babe, can you tell me why I have this huge charge on my checking account?"

Craig grabbed the phone and looked at her bank account, "Yeah, you overdrew your checking account."

Sheri replied, "I didn't overdraw anything! I still have checks in my checkbook."

Thankfully, their accounts aren't consolidated, and they have time to get on the same page as far as how to best handle their finances. If you are in a similar stage as Craig and Sheri, use the pre-marriage time to talk about finances and how you will handle them as a married couple.

For anyone married, you can do any one of the three options mentioned. More and more married couples choose to either keep their money separate or opt for a hybrid version. With more and more women in the workforce, there is less dependency on the man or one spouse being the sole breadwinner. This is great for the families financially, but when it comes time for who to pay, you will need to have a solid plan that works for everyone.

Here are the definitions of each method followed by their pros and cons:

Separate: Each individual maintains separate accounts.

Pros:
- A more equitable sharing process. Even if your incomes are vastly different, you can share expenses using percentages.
- Maintain financial independence.
- Ease of uncoupling.

Cons:
- Inconvenient in paying joint expenses.
- It doesn't prevent arguments over philosophical differences for handling money.

If you decide to keep your finances separate, I suggest you discuss money and your beliefs on spending. Come up with a plan for splitting expenses, or perhaps a scenario such as, you pay these bills, and I'll pay those bills.

Joint: A merging of all finances

Pros:
- Ease of bill payments
- No awkwardness of who pays for what.

Cons:
- Lack of financial independence.
- You are now tied into a partner's poor financial decisions.
- How you each handle money can be a source of conflict.
- Typically, one person holds all the finances, which is unfair on both ends.
- Uncoupling is more difficult.

Joining finances is a good idea if you are married, agree on goals, have similar beliefs around handling money, and want the ease of bill payments. Joining funds is the more traditional approach, and many couples still use this method successfully. But it all comes down to open communication and consensus around how money is spent and saved—without that, you're looking for trouble.

Hybrid: A mix of joint and separate, where there are joint accounts to take care of bills and individual accounts for personal spending and saving.

Pros:
- Ease of bill payments.
- No awkwardness of who pays for what.
- Maintain your financial independence.

Cons:
- For this plan to work, there must be a clearly defined set of rules around what gets paid out of the joint accounts and how much each partner contributes to the joint accounts.
- Not as easy to uncouple as separate accounts. If you decide to break up and both have access to certain accounts, it could become a contention point.

In the hybrid version, you will have joint accounts for the sake of covering your living expenses, such as a checking account, charge card, and savings account. This money will be designated for housing, food, insurance, cars, and savings. For those extraneous purchases, each will maintain money in separate accounts. This method would work well for those who have different beliefs when it comes to finances (The Pros and Cons of a Joint Bank Account).

Takeaway: Just as you don't expect your doctor to come up with a treatment for your health without knowing your symptoms, neither should you or your partner develop a financial plan without knowing all the facts and understanding each other's views.

So, take the following steps when contemplating financial arrangements:

- Be clear on the facts of each of your financial situations.
- Discuss your beliefs and ideas around spending and saving money.
- Determine how to proceed as to separate accounts, joint accounts, or go with a hybrid approach.
- Establish short-term and long-term goals.
- Make sure that you both are active in monitoring your accounts.
- Revisit your finances frequently to be sure you are on track and in agreement.

Remember, like sex, finances can be a significant source of conflict or just a tiny solidifying part of your relationship. It's all in the approach. Be honest and carry through with your plans with respect for one another and your union.

Myth #45: A woman who earns more can be threatening to a male partner

Women aren't staying barefoot and pregnant in the kitchen anymore. More and more women are in the workforce in today's world, with almost a third earning more than their husbands. And why does it matter? Because old traditions and stereotypes, wherein the man should be the breadwinner or be the one who always pays, still governs some men's way of thinking.

Along with earnings, the change in household responsibilities is also changing. Women who work outside the home need a partner to help with the duties inside the house. Studies, funny enough, have shown that men help more than before, but women will still do more than men despite working the same hours outside the home. It's not until the woman starts to make close to, or more than the man, that the man begins to change his tune and pick up the slack. Hmmm, that's a curious phenomenon.

But if we look at the young couples of today, many were raised in the traditional home, where even though Mom may have had a job, Dad was the primary breadwinner. And Mom, in those homes, still carried the workload inside the house as well. So, although we see a shift of more women making more and men increasing their contribution to household responsibilities, the ties back to the traditional roles still exist.

In the end, if you are both working outside the home, how much you bring in is irrelevant. If your wife is a social worker, working 12-hour days, and you are a contractor working 10 hours a day, but you bring in far more than your wife, does any of that matter? No, it does not. Household chores and helping raise the children should be an equal responsibility.

I heard a story about a family that got relocated from the US to Canada. The man worked for a successful start-up and made a good living. His wife was a stay-at-home mom. He worked long hours, and one night, to his family's surprise, he arrived home earlier than usual. His wife asked if he would help bathe the kids. The husband replied, "You have your job, and I have mine." Let's just say the rest of the night went downhill after that comment.

Takeaway: When I talk to couples, I always stress that they should approach their marriage and family as a team. It's not about tit for tat, but about getting things done so that they can have a happy home. Is a perfect 50/50 split attainable? Probably not for every aspect, but you can try and get as close as possible. Remember, you may give more on some things, and your spouse may give more on others. In the end, it is all about what works for you as an individual and what works for your family.

In this fast-paced modern life, we need to adapt our lives to the current environment and dispense with limiting stereotypes. If your wife brings in more money than you, should it matter? No. If you are a team, as I said, then the end goals are where you should focus your attention. If you allow old habits to creep into your head, you could jeopardize your family. Remember what's important. It's not about who makes the dough, just that you have it to keep your family fed and a shelter over their heads.

Chapter 9 - Final Take-aways

Do you remember Build-a-Bear? As a child, you would go into one of their stores and stuff and dress your teddy bear. You got to design the perfect cuddly companion to take home. Well, imagine that same concept concerning finding a romantic partner. I bet some of you are horrified, while others are like, "Wait, that's not a bad idea." But aren't we doing that already between social media and dating apps? Aren't we attempting to find the perfect mate based on physical appearance and a resume of sorts?

Recently, a man I know, we will call him Joe, met a nice woman online and arranged to meet her at a local arboretum to walk and talk. He shows up and waits by the entrance. His phone rings, and it's her. "Hey, I'm here at the entrance," he says.

"Yeah, I know. Turn around," she replies.

Joe did turn around, and he explained to me just how shocked he had been that this woman was drastically different than the picture on her profile. "She looked older and about 100 pounds heavier. Not that I'm looking for perfection, but she looked nothing like the woman I saw on the app. Shouldn't people represent themselves more accurately?"

My answer to that was an emphatic, "Yes! But they don't."

Joe asked, "Why? I'm not a great-looking guy, but I put my picture out there. It is what it is, as they say."

"Joe, people don't advertise the truth because they don't like their truth. They are not comfortable in their skin. Stay away from those individuals, not because you don't like what they look like, but because they aren't secure in themselves."

There are two schools of thought floating in the universe. First, some say that people have to doctor things a little. Otherwise, no one will be interested. While the other side believes that if someone doesn't like the "real" you, they aren't worth your time. Forget the content of what these statements say and ask: What are both of these statements focused on? They are focused on the reaction of someone else. When you want a romantic partner, should you be looking outward or inward? Here's a clue: Love doesn't start with others; it begins with you.

You can't be happy or comfortable with anyone until you are comfortable with yourself. There is a Whitney Houston song titled, "The Greatest Love of All." While watching an episode of *"How it Really Happened,"* with Hill Harper yesterday, I heard that song. A line in the song goes something like, "Learning to love yourself, it is the greatest love of all." The power in that message far exceeded Whitney's incredible voice and exemplified my point perfectly: Self-love enables you to give and receive love from the right sources effectively.

If I were to sum the previous chapters up in one sentence, all roads to romantic happiness lead back to you. Strong romantic relationships start by looking inward. Understanding and acknowledging who you are and what you need is essential before changing your Facebook status from single to unavailable.

As humans, we project to the world what we feel inside. If you feel bad about yourself, you will project that negativity. And what you put out there is what you tend to attract. If you are an emotional mess, you will not attract someone stable, confident, and who shares your values. You will attract someone who is most likely insecure and may exploit your weaknesses. For example, when individuals are insecure about themselves, any attention they get is welcomed. Those who seek to exploit someone with a weakness seek out insecure individuals like a guided missile to its target. Narcissists, for example, don't go after self-assured people because they will be exposed for their wrongdoings. Instead, they go for the meek and mild persons who won't stand up for themselves.

"Love is a two-way street constantly under construction."
- *Carroll Bryant*

Here are the key things you must do if you want to obtain and keep a healthy, loving relationship:

Self-Love: I always think of that famous line from *Jerry McGuire* when Tom Cruise shows up at Renee Zellweger's house and utters, "You, complete, me." Sure, everyone wants to feel like they are the center of someone else's universe—it can make you feel good about yourself, appreciated. But do you want that responsibility? Or should you place that burden on someone else? No, neither works. The idea of someone "completing" another person is for romantic movies only.

If you have low self-esteem and don't feel good about yourself, think about who would be attracted to that. It won't be that confident guy or woman who wants a genuine romantic partnership. Nope. You could instead end up with someone insecure like yourself. And that someone will exploit your insecurities to cover their own. If we look honestly at the movie *Jerry McGuire*, both main characters were a hot mess. And didn't Tom Cruise's character take advantage of Renee's character's insecurity to feed his failing ego? Think about it. Is that a healthy relationship? It makes for an iconic movie ending, but it wouldn't work out in real life.

So, how do you get to that point of knowing and loving yourself? Here are some starting points:

- It all begins with honesty. You need to identify areas you need to work on physically, emotionally, and psychologically. And no, I don't mean you need to look like some skinny supermodel.
- Address the things you can change about yourself that you don't feel good about. If you need to feel better physically, come up with a plan to eat better or exercise more. If you hate your profession, figure out what you are passionate about and go after it.
- Set goals and hold yourself accountable for meeting them. Remember always to make your goals measurable and attainable.
- Once you've reached your goal, reward yourself and then set another goal. Goal setting is an iterative process that will lead to high performance in all areas of your life. This will be transformative and essential to self-love.
- More importantly, you need to learn to love yourself for those things you can't change. For example, you may hate how short your legs are.

Instead of seeing all the things that only look good on tall people, start looking for those things that work for your height. Start seeing the advantages in all the parts of you, instead of the disadvantages.

- Take negative words out of your vocabulary when talking about yourself. Don't say, "Oh, I'm just a cashier." Embrace who you are and be proud of the work you do. Say, "I'm a cashier at Target." Be definitive in your words and own your narrative!

Individuals who have self-love generally command respect. Notice, I used the word "command" and not "demand." Those who demand respect are insecure. If you command it, you get it naturally because of the confidence and security you project. You don't take yourself too seriously, but you know your worth. You also give others respect, and you associate with others who do the same.

Self-love and self-acceptance will take away your need for someone else to "complete you." This process takes time, and it looks different for every person. But, take the time to know yourself and love yourself before looking for that special person to share your life with. It's not about attracting Mr. or Mrs. Right, but about you being Mr. or Mrs. Right. Just as the airlines tell us, take care of yourself first, then turn to others.

Expectations: If you are a self-assured single ready to mingle, how do you move forward? Don't expect perfection, nor should you dumb down your wants. Instead, reframe what you want into a realistic desire. Do you want someone to just stare at, or someone who makes you laugh when you want to cry? Think about it.

The couples I see who have the best relationship foundations, share common goals and beliefs. They aren't identical twins, but they can agree on the critical things that matter to them. Make sure you look for someone who can straddle the fence between supporting and challenging you. The right person will share your core values, while introducing you to other aspects of life and pushing you to grow.

Decipher Myths and Motives: As you search for the right one, be open to others' opinions but discriminating. Ask yourself, how does this myth work for me? Does it limit me or my beliefs? Will it make me and possibly my partner happier? Then go back and reread this book. It's a quick read intentionally. I want you to remind yourself once in a while of what was discussed. We all need a little reminder to stay on a good path, right?

Remember, I'm not saying that all myths or the so-called dating rules are wrong and avoid listening to them. Instead, I'm saying to hear the advice from family and friends, but ask yourself: What is the motive behind what's being said? I am not suggesting that family and friends are all diabolical in their intentions. I am suggesting, however, that their efforts may not be serving your overall objectives. In their attempt to offer support, your loved ones may lead you down an incorrect path—listen objectively.

Effective Communication: Communicate your wants, your needs, but also listen. Communication encompasses expressing your wants and needs and requires you to listen to your partner's desires too. If you love someone enough to consider them "the one," then you should talk about everything from your physical, emotional, psychological, and financial needs. You matter, but so too does your partner. Having a reliable means of communication will feed your connection, which is the key to staying in love. Once you've found the one and begin to reveal more of your authentic self, remain true to yourself. Be sure to communicate with respect and listen to your partner's side of things. Remember, a relationship is two individuals coming together to form one unit. You don't lose your individuality, but you gain a combined union.

Connections: Then, once you've found the one, keep that connection alive. It's not always going to be like those first sparks, and that's a good thing. Those first sparks, yes, are exciting, and you feel all that tingling inside, but there is nothing better than knowing your life partner has your back no matter what. That they will be there to support you, good or bad, and that you can share your life fully with this person. Those feelings blow the new love feelings out of the water and over the moon.

The connection needs to be tended to like a garden. Even if you just steal a few minutes throughout the day to get back to one another, it will feed that connection. And as I said, if your relationship is strong, then your communication will flow easier. And the more you communicate authentically with each other, the better you will enhance your connection—the circle of love. Keep that circle tight and robust, and even gale-force winds won't break it.

There are many facets to creating a solid foundation for a long-lasting relationship. I've debunked the myths that I hear in both my personal and professional life. I can't encourage you enough to follow the steps I've laid out for you here. But I also encourage anyone who needs help to talk to a professional. From time to time, we all need guidance, and successful individuals know when to ask for help. Be that person. If you're struggling, get help from a qualified individual—It's an act of self-love.

The other day, my three o'clock pang hit, and I needed my caffeine fix. I rolled into my usual shop and noticed a new girl behind the counter.

"Hi," I said.

Seemingly flustered, the girl said, "How can I help you?"

"I'd like a large coffee. Your special roast is fine." She proceeded to stare at the coffee pots with confusion. "Is everything ok?" I asked while checking my watch.

She turned and looked at me, her eyes filled with tears, "I'm sorry. It's just that the last guy that came in asked for a coffee, and I didn't put the lid on tight enough. It spilled all over him."

"Accidents happen. I wouldn't worry about it," I said attempting to comfort her. She smiled and then went to fill my cup.

The bell on the door rang, and I turned around to see a male customer walk up behind me wearing a suit with a weird orange shirt underneath his suit coat. And he was already holding a cup in his hand. The barista turned back around with my cup. I reached for it, but she pulled it back with a shocked look on her face. Confused, I looked back and forth between her and the customer behind me.

"I can take my coffee now," I said, reaching for it again.

"Oh, I'm sorry." She handed me the coffee and then looked at the guy behind me and repeated herself, "Oh, I'm so sorry."

I stepped out of the way and went over to the table with the cream and sugar.

The guy stepped up to the counter, "Oh, no worries. I got a new shirt from the card shop next door." He exposed a new, bright orange t-shirt that read "Live, Laugh, and Love."

"Oh, I'm sorry. Do you have to wear that all day?" The embarrassed barista asked.

"I don't mind. But would you pour me another cup?"

The barista looked excited to redeem herself, "Oh, yes!"

"Can you do me a favor this time?"

The barista cocked her head to one side, "Put the lid on tight this time?"

"Yes, and write your name and number on the cup? I'd like to take you out to dinner sometime."

I walked out as the two were knee-deep in conversation and smiled to myself, thinking how much luck and openness play a role in finding someone. Someone I knew used to tell me, "There's a lid for every pot," and I believe it's true. That day I may have witnessed a pot finding its lid, and it perked my day up far beyond the coffee—a first for me.

Check Lists/Critical Points

Looking for Love:

- ❏ Love yourself first
- ❏ Look for someone to enhance your life, but don't expect them to make your life
- ❏ Frame expectations with a realistic outlook and a focus on what truly matters
- ❏ Love isn't easy. It will take some effort
- ❏ Be open and honest, don't play games
- ❏ Look for individuals who share your values and beliefs
- ❏ Age shouldn't be a factor in dating

New Relationships:

- ❏ Listen to advice from family and friends, but filter information by understanding motives
- ❏ Discuss your parameters concerning access to each other's lives
- ❏ Jealousy never equals love
- ❏ Love is not all a relationship needs to succeed
- ❏ Relationships need love, trust, communication, connection, and a willingness to work
- ❏ Only share prior sexual encounters when:
    - Unprotected sex occurred
    - If you had sex within your or your partner's social group

Committed Relationships:

- ❏ Living together is an individual decision; make it for all the right reasons. Do not rush any part of your relationship progression
- ❏ There will never be a perfect 50/50 split of responsibilities, but you can get close with open communication
- ❏ Communicate your needs but do it respectfully and when your partner is most open to listening

❏ Do not avoid arguments

❏ Keep arguments constructive by practicing empathy and being open

❏ Take care of yourself physically and emotionally for yourself and your partner

Marriage:

❏ Only you and your loved one decide when you should get married

❏ Compromise is not the answer; find a win-win resolution is

❏ If you are connected, you will communicate better

❏ People don't change unless they want to. Marriage won't make your partner better

❏ Do not employ peace at any price

❏ Marriage should be your top priority, as it's the foundation of your family

❏ Babies make marriage harder, not easier

❏ Relationships shouldn't take you on emotional rollercoaster rides

❏ Define parameters around sensitive topics

❏ Forgiveness shouldn't include forgetting

❏ Don't argue when you're sleep-deprived

❏ Staying together should only happen if it means creating a home filled with love and respect

❏ Staying in a bad relationship to avoid loneliness isn't the answer

❏ Don't expect anyone to change

❏ Internal reflection will help you control your responses

❏ Time doesn't heal. It dulls the pain

❏ Your partner is not your punching bag

Finances:

- ❏ Always be prepared to pay your share
- ❏ Openly discuss the finances in a relationship
- ❏ It's best to keep your finances separate until marriage
- ❏ Who earns how much shouldn't matter if you have a loving and supportive marriage

Notes:

Myths Index

Index

Page 22 (2009, March). To Be 'Good Enough'. Retrieved from https://www.ncbi.nlm.nih.gov/pmc/articles/PMC2654842/.

Page 23 Gottman, John, Ph.D. (n.d.). The 3 Phases of Love. Retrieved from https://www.gottman.com/blog/the-3-phases-of-love/

Page 28 Smith, Martin J. (2017, January 17). Turns Out That Opposites Don't Attract After All. Retrieved from https://www.gsb.stanford.edu/insights/turns-out-opposites-dont-attract-after-all

Page 28 Swami, Viren (2017, March 28). Most of us Tend to be Attracted to People Who Are Similar to Ourselves. Retrieved from https://www.psypost.org/2017/03/us-tend-attracted-people-similar-48596

Page 43 Wilser, Jeff (2013, July 8). Sex on the First Date. Retrieved from https://www.cosmopolitan.com/sex-love/advice/a4546/dont-have-sex-on-the-first-date/

Page 43 (2017, February 6). Singles in America: Match Releases Largest Study on U.S. Single Population. Retrieved from https://match.mediaroom.com/2017-02-06-Singles-in-America-Match-Releases-Largest-Study-on-U-S-Single-Population

Page 51 Curtis, Sophie (2013, September 10). Men Twice as Likely to Mobile Snoop than Women. Retrieved from https://www.telegraph.co.uk/technology/news/10298731/Men-twice-as-likely-to-mobile-snoop-than-women.html

Page 59 Rosenfeld, Michael J. and Roesler, Katharina (2018, September 24). Cohabitation Experience and Cohabitation's Association with Marital Dissolution. Retrieved from https://onlinelibrary.wiley.com/doi/abs/10.1111/jomf.12530?af=R&

Page 60 Geiger, A. W., and Livingston, Gretchen (2019, February 13). 8 Facts About Love and Marriage in America. Retrieved from https://www.pewresearch.org/fact-tank/2019/02/13/8-facts-about-love-and-marriage/

Page 61 (2009, March). To Be 'Good Enough'. Retrieved from https://www.ncbi.nlm.nih.gov/pmc/articles/PMC2654842/.

Page 69 Wang, Wendy (2020, September 9). The Share of Never-Married Americans Has Reached a New High. Retrieved from https://ifstudies.org/blog/the-share-of-never-married-americans-has-reached-a-new-high#:~:-

text=of%20Americans%20marry.-,In%202018%2C%20a%20record%20 35%25%20of%20Americans%20ages%2025%20to,to%20fall%20during%20 a%20recession

Page 70 Wolfinger, Nicholas H. (2015, July 20). Replicating the Goldilocks Theory of Marriage and Divorce. Retrieved from https://ifstudies.org/blog/ replicating-the-goldilocks-theory-of-marriage-and-divorce/

Page 70 Luscombe, Belinda (2015, July21). Math Says This Is the Perfect Age to Get Married. Retrieved from https://time.com/3966588/marriage-wed-ding-best-age/

Page 94 Ferreira, Charity (December 12, 2019). 8 Tips for Forgiving Someone Who Hurt You. Retrieved from https://stanfordmag.org/contents/8-tips-for-forgiving-someone-who-hurt-you

Page 99 Bowcott, Owen (2015, November 22). Children of Divorce: 82% Rather Parents Separate than 'Stay for the Kids'. Retrieved from https://www. theguardian.com/lifeandstyle/2015/nov/22/children-divorce-resolution-sur-vey-rather-parents-separate

Page 111 Lever, Janet, Frederick, David A., and Hertz, Roseanna (2015, No-vember 5). Who Pays for Dates?. Retrieved from https://journals.sagepub. com/doi/10.1177/2158244015613107

Page 113 Gjelten, E.A. (n.d.). What Causes Divorce? 8 Common Reasons Marriages End. Retrieved from https://www.divorcenet.com/resources/com-mon-reasons-marriages-end.html

Page 114-115 (n.d.). The Pros and Cons of a Joint Bank Account. Retrieved from https://www.centralbank.net/learning-center/the-pros-and-cons-of-a-joint-bank-account/

Made in United States
North Haven, CT
04 October 2023

42369401R00074